OTHER VOLUMES IN THIS SERIES

THE

BEST

AMERICAN

POETRY

2008

◇   ◇   ◇

Charles Wright, Editor

David Lehman, Series Editor

SCRIBNER POETRY

NEW YORK   LONDON   TORONTO   SYDNEY

SCRIBNER POETRY
A Division of Simon & Schuster, Inc.
1230 Avenue of the Americas
New York, NY 10020

First Scribner edition September 2008

SCRIBNER POETRY *and design are registered trademarks of The Gale Group, Inc.,*
used under license by Simon & Schuster, Inc., the publisher of this work.

For information about special discounts for bulk purchases,
please contact Simon & Schuster Special Sales at 1-800-456-6798
or business@simonandschuster.com

Manufactured in the United States of America

1   3   5   7   9   10   8   6   4   2

Library of Congress Control Number: 88644281

ISBN-13: 978-0-7432-9974-9
ISBN-10: 0-7432-9974-4
ISBN-13: 978-0-7432-9975-6 (Pbk)
ISBN-10: 0-7432-9975-2 (Pbk)

CONTENTS

David Lehman was born in New York City in 1948. He was educated at Columbia University and spent two years in England as a Kellett Fellow at Cambridge University. *When a Woman Loves a Man* (Scribner, 2005) is the most recent of his seven books of poetry. He has edited *The Oxford Book of American Poetry* (Oxford University Press, 2006) and *The Best American Erotic Poems: From 1800 to the Present* (Scribner, 2008). He has written five nonfiction books, including *The Last Avant-Garde: The Making of the New York School of Poets* (Doubleday Anchor, 1999) and *The Perfect Murder: A Study in Detection* (University of Michigan Press, 2000). He teaches in the graduate writing program of the New School in New York City. He initiated the *Best American Poetry* series in 1988.

FOREWORD

by David Lehman

◇　◇　◇

In a wonderful essay in *The Dyer's Hand* (1962)—an essay written far in advance of the ubiquitous writing workshop—W. H. Auden prescribed the curriculum of his "daydream College for Bards." Matriculated students in the "daydream college" must learn at least one ancient and two modern languages. They have to memorize thousands of lines of verse. Forbidden from reading criticism, they must exercise their critical faculties by writing parodies. They need to take courses in prosody, rhetoric, and comparative philology. Most unconventionally, they are required to study three subjects from a varied group, including "archaeology, mythology, liturgics, cooking," and they are expected also to take up gardening or to adopt a four-legged pet.

While the proposed banning of literary criticism from the college library may go too far, I think Auden is right about a lot of things. The value of knowing a poem by heart lies not in the public recitation but in the inward recollection of the lines when one is in a vacant or a pensive mood; there is simply no better way to possess a poem than to memorize it. A good parody is an act of practical criticism, as instructive and more amusing than most. Among the most efficacious exercises are those that involve writing in set forms and handling various metrical and stanzaic patterns. I agree, too, on the value of such nonliterary activities as cooking and gardening, which in their creative processes and structures bear more than a passing resemblance to the act of writing. Given the sheer number of graduate writing programs in the country today—urban or pastoral, low or high residency, fancy or no frills, traditional or innovative—it's a wonder, in a way, that none has given Auden's curriculum a try.

Auden begins "The Poet & the City" with the observation that a great many young people of limited talent, "when asked what they want to do in life," answer neither sensibly ("I want to be a lawyer, an innkeeper, a farmer") nor romantically ("I want to be an explorer, a racing motorist, a missionary, President of the United States"). Instead they want to become writers, "creative" writers. The phenomenon had long astonished and vexed the author. In "The Prolific and the Devourer," written in 1939, the year Auden first took up residence in America, he asserts that the secret meaning of "I want to write" is "I don't want to work." Art as a form of play, he adds, "is the least dependent on the good-will of others and looks the easiest." For the shirkers, Auden's message is that you must work very hard not only at becoming a poet but at earning a living. He goes on to recommend learning a craft or taking up a trade that does not "involve the manipulation of words," a very Audenesque piece of advice that his own industrious practice as an essayist and anthologist belies. Perhaps, to paraphrase Oscar Wilde, the only thing to do with good advice is pass it on and assume that it doesn't apply to you. Richard Howard, the guest editor of the 1995 volume in this series, recollects the time that "Wystan [Auden's first name] scolded me for translating books from the French. He thought manual labor was a much more suitable idea." On another occasion, Auden voiced his opinion that "poets should dress like businessmen," while he wore, in James Schuyler's words, "an incredible peach / -colored nylon shirt."

Such inconsistencies are amusing but do not affect the central point, and we may thank Auden for raising the whole question of what job options there are for, in his phrase, "the average poet." Many young writers today can see their lives unfold in a seamless transition from one side of the classroom to the other without an intervening period of living in the place that professors sometimes call the "quote-unquote real world." The importance of going out into the world and encountering its complexity and range of possibility is surely one thing we might stress in our latter-day College for Bards.

The proliferation of graduate, degree-granting writing programs in the thirty-five years since Auden's death may not have surprised one so suspicious of the vanity of young writers. Yet even a critic of the workshop structure, centering as it does on the student rather than on canonical texts, might welcome the news that MFA programs continue to flourish—if only because writing requires reading and because we may owe to these programs the perpetuation of the art that we practice and the "influences" we honor and sometimes contend with like uncles and aunts and grandparents. The Association of Writing Programs (AWP) held its annual conference in New York City in 2008, and the sold-out event, attracting more participants and book exhibits than any in the organization's history, was nothing if not a sign of a profession in vigorous health. In undergraduate education, too, creative writing has become a vital force. The Association of Departments of English (ADE), a branch of the Modern Languages Association (MLA), periodically takes up a recurrent problem: the decline in the percentage of undergraduates majoring in English.[1] In response to the predicament, a number of English departments have expanded their offerings in creative writing. This has proved a shrewd maneuver. The success of the gambit attests not just to the lure of self-expression but to the assertion of the pleasure principle in matters of art and literature. Who would not choose the pleasure of making narratives and lyrics if the alternative is to "problematize a text"?

We who teach writing know how pure and strong the literary impulse remains among our students. We are impressed with their ambition and their commitment. But we know also that reading and writing exist in a symbiotic relationship, and many of us wonder how it came about that even some of our most talented and energetic young writers got through college with having read so little. When I wrote *Signs of the Times: Deconstruction and the Fall of Paul de Man* (1991), the joke in currency was that if you crossed a mafioso and a deconstructionist, what you got was someone who makes you "an offer that you can't understand." The beauty of the joke was that it did three things at once: it confirmed the iconic status of *The Godfather*; it made the point that jargon and abstruse terminology result in incomprehensible prose; and it attributed a mob mentality to a clique that was reputedly skillful, even ruthless, at the academic game of chutes and tenure ladders. I worried then that the hegemony of critical theory may serve to rationalize and would probably accelerate the neglect of authors and the decay of practical criticism. It gives the maker of that prediction little satisfaction to see it come true.

Something larger than the ideological and political conflicts between and within academic departments is at stake here. In the real culture war, the war for the survival of the literary culture, the dummies seem to be

1. See, for example, "The Undergraduate English Major," the report of the 2001–2002 ADE Ad Hoc Committee on the English Major, which was formed to study "the recent decline in the number of English majors and recommend ways in which departments can address the decline and its possible underlying causes." The committee affirms that "curricular changes inside English departments are not, as some would claim, a primary factor responsible for the flight of students from English—a flight that can seem an educational disaster" but isn't if you take the long view. *ADE Bulletin,* no. 134–135, Spring–Fall 2003, pp. 68–91.

winning. There are days when even an unflagging champion of the written word may fear that his or her best efforts may turn out to have the same effect as a prayer to the patron saint of lost causes. The force against literacy in the old-fashioned sense of reading books, understanding traditions, and recollecting history is, in the old-fashioned sense, awesome. In 2004 the National Endowment for the Arts issued its grim report *Reading at Risk,* and a year ago the NEA followed up with *To Read or Not to Read.* The reports make the case that "reading skills" correlate directly to individual achievement and career success, not to mention the health of the culture and the education of the citizenry. And by all standards, we are failing. The percentage of the U.S. population that reads books went down from an estimated 61 percent in 1992 to under 57 percent ten years later. That's a slow but steady rate of decline. There's little surprise and less comfort in learning that the rate of decline is faster when it comes to works of fiction and poetry. Between 1982 and 2002, the percentage of the population that had read a "creative" book in the previous twelve months went down from 56.9 to 46.7. "More alarming [than the decline in newspaper circulation and in household spending on books] are indications that Americans are losing not just the will to read but even the ability," Caleb Crain writes in *The New Yorker.* Crain summarizes the view of some sociologists that reading books for pleasure may someday become "an increasingly arcane hobby."[2] If one culprit among many is television, one effect is the "dumbing down" of culture—a trend so powerful it brought a new phrase into currency. People know astoundingly little about, say, American history, and this (they think) is no big deal. Every now and then an author risks being called a "curmudgeon" or a "crank" for airing misgivings about this state of affairs, while indulging the guilty pleasure of circulating anecdotes of epic American ignorance. Patricia Cohen's *New York Times* piece on Susan Jacoby's book *The Age of American Unreason* begins with the "adorable platinum blonde" who thought that Europe was a country. She was a contestant on the FOX game show *Are You Smarter Than a 5th Grader?*—the whole premise of which is that Americans are stupider than ever and reveling in it. Jacoby herself says she wrote her book because (in Cohen's paraphrase) "anti-intellectualism (the attitude that 'too much learning can be a dangerous thing') and anti-rationalism ('the idea that there is no such things as evidence or fact, just opinion') have fused in a particularly insidious

2. Caleb Crain, "The Twilight of the Books" in *The New Yorker,* December 24 & 31, 2007, pp. 134–135.

way." Jacoby's immediate trigger was an overheard conversation in which one well-dressed man told another that "Pearl Harbor" "was when the Vietnamese dropped bombs in a harbor, and it started the Vietnam War."[3]

In the teeth of an epidemic of ignorance, we must decide what and how to teach the young people who come to us convinced that they have a poetic vocation. We should encourage them to read widely—to read everything they can. But we should assuredly not mock anyone for what they do not know or have not yet read. Rather, respond with ardor to their list of unread books: for though rereading is a great art, nothing can beat the first time you live with *Crime and Punishment* or Keats's odes and letters or Genesis or Homer or Dante or Emily Dickinson or Byron's *Don Juan*. It's a list-maker's delight, devising the syllabus for a course on, say, what Keats called the "vale of soul-making"—the making of a poet. We may take as our motto this line from Ben Jonson's ode to the memory of Shakespeare: "For a good poet's made, as well as born." On my syllabus I'd include some of the aforementioned works, as well as Emerson's essays, Gertrude Stein's lectures and *The Autobiography of Alice B. Toklas*, Wordsworth's *Prelude*, and Rilke's *Letters to a Young Poet*. What, gentle reader, would you choose?

Our obligations to our students do not stop at texts and assignments, instruction on the preparation of a manuscript, information about the literary marketplace, methods of dealing with writer's block, models for how to disagree without resort to fisticuffs. By our example we can prove that a conversation or debate about poetry need not reflect the corrosive nature of the national political discourse. There is also the need for students—for all of us, really—to come to terms with the likelihood of rejection and the inevitability of injustice. Someday someone else in the room will win the award or the fellowship or the honor that *you* deserved. But envy is always an error, and to win a prize or an award is not the reason you wrote poetry in the first place. Return to that original impulse. Don't give in to resentment and bitterness, the enemies of poetry. We could probably devote an entire course in the "daydream College" to one aphorism from Auden's prologue to *The Dyer's Hand*: "No poet or novelist wishes he were the only one who ever lived, but most of them wish they were the only one alive, and quite a number fondly believe their wish has been granted."[4]

3. Patricia Cohen, "Dumb and Dumber: Are Americans Hostile to Knowledge?" *The New York Times,* February 14, 2008.

4. Auden, *The Dyer's Hand* (Vintage, 1962, 1989), p. 14.

When the *Best American Poetry* series was new, I would use this space to explain our rules and procedures. Years have gone by since I last explained that each year a different guest editor, himself or herself a distinguished poet, chooses the seventy-five poems in a volume, and that usually the seventy-five poems are by as many poets, though there have been exceptions (1996 and 2007, for example). It's unwise to take too much for granted, and it can't hurt to reiterate here that we construe "American" as broadly as possible, counting resident aliens and temporary residents (if the guest editor feels passionately about the poem) and routinely including Canadian poets. Since the 1991 volume, poems have been chosen exclusively from print or electronic magazines and periodicals, not from individual books, collections, or anthologies. Translations are ineligible. The poets are asked to comment on their poems, and the majority of them do so, transforming the genre of contributors' notes from an afterthought into a feature of the anthology that many readers find particularly valuable. The guest editor makes the selections and contributes an introductory essay; the series editor contributes a foreword, works with the guest editor in ways that vary from year to year, and assembles the manuscript. The guest editor's decisions are final and definitive.

Undoubtedly the most important decision we have to make annually is the identity of the person who will put his or her stamp on a volume in a series that chronicles the taste of our leading practitioners. Honored among his peers, Charles Wright seemed a natural for this editorial job and brought a keen sense of responsibility to it. He worked hard to be ecumenical, balancing the desire to be inclusive with the unrelenting need to favor excellence. Born in Pickwick Dam, Tennessee, Wright discovered his poetic vocation while serving in U.S. Army Intelligence in Italy in the 1950s. After completing four years of active duty, he left the army in 1961 and soon was studying with Donald Justice at the University of Iowa. Since 1983 Wright has taught at the University of Virginia. His poetry has a spiritual, even a religious flavor—"each line is a station of the cross," he has said—though it calls to mind a religion based on doubt more than faith. In a poem in *Scar Tissue* (2006), Wright depicts himself as a song and dance man—but one who has the west wind whistling and Dante's souls dancing in his brain. The urge to pray outlasts the conviction that God will hear the prayer. Yet the capital G in the opening phrase of this arresting passage performs a little miracle of poetic transformation:

A God-fearing agnostic,

            I tend to look in the corners of things,

Those out-of-the-way places,

The half-dark and half-hidden,

            the passed-by and over-looked,

Whenever I want to be sure I can't find something.

As this excerpt from "Confessions of a Song and Dance Man" illustrates, Wright has a distinctive way of breaking his lines in the middle: the second half begins where the first left off, one line space lower on the page. The device in his hands is a potent means of punctuating space, as well suited to his poetic pursuits as A. R. Ammons's colons are to his project of "colonizing" the known universe.

The year 2007 was favorable for guest editors past and present of *The Best American Poetry*. Charles Simic, who edited *The Best American Poetry 1992*, succeeded Donald Hall (*BAP 1989*) as U.S. poet laureate. (Counting Simic, seven *Best American Poetry* guest editors have held the post.) During that same week in August, the Academy of American Poets announced that Simic had won this year's prestigious Wallace Stevens Award. Robert Hass (*BAP 2001*) garnered the National Book Award and a Pulitzer for *Time and Materials*. Paul Muldoon (*BAP 2005*) became poetry editor of *The New Yorker*. John Ashbery (*BAP 1988*) was named poet laureate of MTV. And the 2007 Griffin Prize went to Charles Wright for *Scar Tissue*.

On February 14, 2008, Scribner published *The Best American Erotic Poems: From 1800 to the Present*. On the same day, an assistant principal of a high school in Springfield, Ohio, was suspended (and was eventually obliged to resign) when school officials learned he had posted erotic poems on the net under the pseudonym Antonio Love. This all happened (the local newscast reported) "after a parent complained about the alleged poetry." (The *alleged* there is a final twist of the knife.) Who says that hot poems can't get you into trouble in 2008? Poetry remains a bad influence all these years after Plato banished the poets from his ideal republic.

Charles Wright was born in Pickwick Dam, Tennessee, in 1935. Educated at Davidson College in North Carolina, he served in U.S. Army Intelligence for four years, then attended the University of Iowa Writers' Workshop. *Chickamauga*, his eleventh collection of poems, won the 1996 Lenore Marshall Poetry Prize. A year later, *Black Zodiac* (Farrar, Straus and Giroux, 1997) was awarded the Pulitzer Prize and the *Los Angeles Times* Book Prize. His other books include *Scar Tissue* (Farrar, Straus and Giroux, 2006), *Buffalo Yoga* (2004), *Negative Blue* (2000), *Appalachia* (1998), *The World of the Ten Thousand Things: Poems 1980–1990*, *Zone Journals* (1988), and *Country Music: Selected Early Poems* (1983). He has two volumes of criticism in the University of Michigan Press's Poets on Poetry Series: *Halflife* (1988) and *Quarter Notes* (1995). His translation of Eugenio Montale's *The Storm and Other Poems* (1978) received the PEN Translation Prize. In 1999 he was elected a Chancellor of the Academy of American Poets. He is Souder Family Professor of English at the University of Virginia in Charlottesville.

INTRODUCTION

by Charles Wright

◇   ◇   ◇

IMPROVISATIONS ON PROFLIGACY AND RESTRAINT

—*"The form is always the measure of the obsession."*
—Alberto Giacometti

—Almost all the pluralities of our current poetries would seem contained in the poem "That Nature Is a Heraclitean Fire and of the Comfort of the Resurrection"—the (relatively) new Elliptical poetry—add Paul Celan, add *Finnegans Wake*—, the (relatively) old Language poetries, the (always) continuous narrative and formal poetries, and the imagistic outriders and cattle herders that for a century now have been in the saddle. Whitman said he contained multitudes. Hopkins did as well but never boasted about it. And probably had a few people more inside him. The Confessionals, for instance—see the Terrible sonnets—whose whines and self-inflictions still ring in our ears. The Black Mountain naturalists (Olson). The Beat naturalists (Snyder).

—It's odd what poetry does for us, and doesn't do. It can save our lives individually, but not collectively. It can move mountains, but not molehills. It can sing, but it can't dance (though the poet can be moved to do so). It can boil blood, but not water. It can comfort, but is no comforter. It is, as they say in Reno, a hard point to make.

—It's difficult to be both clear and emotionally resonant. Perhaps that's one of the reasons the younger generations are anxious to excise emotion and its intensity out of their poems. But cleverness is not what endures. Only pain endures. And the rhythm of pain.

★   ★   ★

—Poetry is the fox under our shirts that gnaws away at our hearts. Outside, we stand firm, inside, we are altered forever.

—Poetry, like high water, floods us from time to time. and then, as the season advances, seeps into us as groundwater, out of whose depths, from time to time, we suck back to the surface, hoping (praying, actually) it's still the same water, and not just the usual runoff. Meanwhile, the heavens clear, the City of Dis opens its gates, and we hang, as we've always hung, between the two, pencil sharpened, nothing to write on but the palms of our hands.

—"When Bill Clinton was inaugurated," Alpert (Herb) said, "they had ten saxophone players at the party. It was mostly the young guns, but Gerry Mulligan was in there, too. Afterward, he called me and said, 'Man, you know, these young guys they know all the modes, they know all the chords, they can play high and low and fast, and they can do amazing things, but the one thing they don't know how to do is leave the bone alone.' "

—Poetry is what's left after the ball is over.

—Outside the windows of our poem, the air is clotted with the images of the invisible, even one of which, could we let it, and it alone, inside, would change our poem, and us, inalterably. But we can't, for the window is sealed for the night, and it's night forever.

—Does anyone talk about form and content anymore? Tenor and vehicle? The rough and the smooth? Language and all its agonized misunderstanding? Here's Roberto Calasso (as translated by Geoffrey Brock) describing the *brahman*, the Hindu sacred ground of being: it is necessarily divided into two parts, the "unmanifest" and the "manifest." The *one* is therefore always *two*. Three fourths of the *brahman* is unmanifest, one fourth manifest. The *brahman*—and here we descend into our own little linguistic mysteries—is the wild goose, which, the texts say (again, according to Calasso), "in rising from the water, it does not extract one foot. If it did, neither today nor tomorrow would exist." The water, he adds, is the unmanifest *brahman*, the goose that rises from it is the manifest. The form, I would add, is that which remains unmanifest, and the content is that which becomes manifest, both still poetry's eternal two in one.

★ ★ ★

—Poems are merely foot movements in a larger dance.

—A word to the wise from Dante in *De Vulgari Eloquentia* (as quoted by James Wright in *The New Naked Poetry*, 1976) " . . . each one ought to take up a subject of such weight as to be a fair burden for his own shoulders, so that their strength may not be too heavily taxed and he be forced to tumble into the mud. This is the advice our master Horace gives us when he says in the beginning of his *Art of Poetry*, 'Ye who write, take up a subject suited to your strength.'"

—What's written down can never be erased.

—Saisho famously wrote, "Before I began studying Zen, I saw mountains as mountains, rivers as rivers. When I learned some Zen, mountains ceased to be mountains, rivers to be rivers. But now, when I have understood Zen, I am in accord with myself and again I see mountains as mountains, rivers as rivers."

—Still, poetry comes, for lack of better words, from the heart (the "foul rag-and-bone-shop of the heart," as Yeats had it), and from the soul— neither a place you can put your finger on, but a place you can surely put your foot in, if you don't watch out. It is a matter of "soul-making," as John Keats said. It truly is *not* a matter of arrangement, of performance, of presentation, of rhetorical dazzle or surprise, though all of those matters may be a part of it. It is *not* the distractions, but the focus. It is not the undercard, but the main event. There is always an emotional half to the equation, but the other half is always craft—you have to be able to say it your way. It's the only time that two plus one makes two—language is half, technique is half, and emotion is half. An emotional value is always involved. Distortions and side events are often interesting and entertaining, but they are *not* the stillness and gathered attention at road's end. It's not a question of paper, of typewriters, of white space or of dark space—it's a question of what's in your life, and where you want that life to lead you. You've only got one, and you can fill it with whatever you want. You're free and American. But if it is poetry that you want, then don't look for language games, intellectual rip-offs, or rhetorical sing-alongs. It's too often been a matter of life and death to those who really cared. You've got to know, in your heart of hearts, that Keats is right, that it is about soul-making, that it does matter, and that it can make you or break you as a person. It is the main event, as I say, and ancillary to nothing. Except music, perhaps, the condition toward which all art constantly strives, as Walter Pater continues to remind us.

> —*"Fail. Fail again. Fail better."*
> —Samuel Beckett

What follows are this year's selections for *The Best American Poetry 2008*. I cast as wide a net as possible to include the best representatives of the various factions and inclinations of American poetry. While I did other things besides read magazines in 2007, it feels as if I have done little else, and these are the poems I liked the most. I chose them with all the feathery weight of the future on their backs. Which weight is equal, more or less, to that of a tear. But as E. M. Cioran tells us, "Only tears will be weighed at the Last Judgment."

★   ★   ★

Now, putting aside my prepared text, I'd like to add a couple of more words. Like most older people—who knows, perhaps all older people—I like things now that I probably wouldn't have liked some forty years ago. And vice versa. I like things to make sense nowadays. Putting aside the nagging possibility that one man's sense is another man's sensibility, as the years wind down, I like a definitiveness in things, I want to understand them, even though I know there is precious little sense in earthly affairs (or unearthly ones, for that matter), and God knows not an unlit wick of understanding. Art is supposed, they say, to make sense out of the senseless, coherence out of the incoherent, and connections out of the unconnectible. And poetry, of course, is an art. Or should be, and not just a rag bag for dusty emotions and stained experiences. Emotional sense, rhythmical sense, rhetorical sense, linguistic sense, musical sense. No posing, no vogueing, no lip-synching. As Stein said to Hemingway, damn it all anyway, remarks are not literature. I don't know how much literature we have in here, but these are some of the things that made some sense to us this year, in one way or another.

★   ★   ★

CODA:

Everyone talks about the "great health" of American poetry nowadays. And it's hard to fault that. There are very few bad poems being published, very few. On the other hand, there are very few really good ones, either, ones that might make you want to stick your fingers in the Cuisinart, saying, Take me now, Lord, take me now. The way I felt about Lowell and Roethke and Berryman back in my green time. And early Creeley and sixties' Merwin. O, there is lots of moving the language around the page (and, I guess, in the mind), there is much whippy, snippy, "gotcha" kind of stuff, alternately interesting, alternately ho-hum. We seem to be in The Great Joyful Swamp of still water and rotting trees, all of the "isms" circled around just ready to have the ground go out from under their feet and add themselves to the watery complacency. We need a kraken to rise up and scare the piss out of us into what's in our hearts and whatever Urge it is that constitutes the soul. We need a non-verbal turbulence, a force, in our poems. We need to have the night and darkness and some real sharp teeth to take the hurly-burly out of our heads and stuff it into our veins. Though Language is always Capo, sometimes we need the Consigliere to whisper in its ear—Time to go to the mattresses, Don Carlo, time for a new poetry *con coglioni*. Let's let the frills and cleverness dance by themselves. Over there, in and among the gum trees. And the water cypress. No more "whatever." Now the sharp blade. After all, it's been a hundred years, you know.

THE
BEST
AMERICAN
POETRY
2008

◇   ◇   ◇

Evening Song

◇   ◇   ◇

The crickets go on with their shrill music.
The sun drops down.

What was it my brother said to me once
in Charleston, before he disappeared that spring
like the quick wake of a water mite?

This was 1980, evening, the porch lights burning.
He was reading from *The Cloud of Unknowing*.

Robins gossiped in the poplars,
moths spiraled across the uncut grass.
Moonlight wormed through the neighboring lawns.

We must therefore pray . . . not in many words,
but in a little word of one syllable.

Didn't he say forgiveness was his homely double?
Didn't he say what I wanted him to say? Maybe
I wasn't listening, chewing a branch of sassafras . . .

But I doubt it. As I doubt, now, that the life
of my lawn is a still life, the moon and shrill chants

opinions on despair. There are times
when the sound the world makes is a little word.
Something like *help*, or *yes* . . .

from *Rivendell*

Exceptions and Melancholies

◇   ◇   ◇

Never before
had we been so thin and so clear
and arranged always
and in the same way gazing and listening
over the rooftops
to tin cans of flowers and strange
music. For an hour or more
I turned the same corner
and felt like a criminal farther and farther out to sea
among the racks of shoes and old clothes
but now looking
back I should never have
unpacked. A street
crowned with chestnut trees
ends at the sewer. You go to a theatre
and find yourself a house
outside the city
and walk the shore
forever. I don't have much
talent for poetry. When I see a wrecking ball
dangling from a crane I mean it
literally. I mean
I don't mean the world's fallen apart
or that a wrecking ball
symbolizes the eye my world-weary sister
couldn't know to turn away
from. The hospital's
exhausted. The little church is boarded up.
We leaned against the limestone

and liked the fact that tea
sweetens gradually
and that the wildflowers
beneath the shade of trees gone shivering
have really livened up the cemetery
and that the tall grass and the garbage
and especially the piled-up
newspapers and the rooftop pool
fit right in among
these windowless buildings
having gathered
as we are in the flesh again
and leading another life
altogether.

from *Runes*

Framing

◇　◇　◇

for Robert Creeley (1926–2005)

What you won't see today:

juniper's tough skein.

★

The rolling
hummocks

have grown syntax—

tassels and bells—

for careless
wings to be among.

★

The tic
in articulation.

★

The present is cupped

by a small effort
of focus—

its muscular surround.

You're left out.

from *The Nation*

Pavane pour Helen Twelvetrees

◊   ◊   ◊

I.

Abrasive chores were a specialty.
Then, suicide at fifty.

Not a back street that didn't reflect
meanness, and somehow, candor.

To be clasped by the awkwardly handsome Phillips Holmes
in an open carriage in Havana:
"St. Patrick's Day, don't it make you feel great?"

There were fiery landladies to cope with
and the usual drunks. Otherwise,
time passes, assuring vulnerability.

I was saying, you never get over
some of these lumps, that's what they're for.
Otherwise, you can abide in discretion,
or just plain bawl.

The clients are coming back. Quick, the moustache cup.

II.

All around us tides, provocation
of abstracted sky and water.
Praise bellies the azaleas. Yeah, praise

them too while we're at it, everything
deserves a modicum of praise, except those
who don't get it. There's more, in a sequel
God will ultimately be writing.

He turns the pages of a vast
octavo volume, brings forefinger
to chin. H'm, that one might have turned out
differently, if I'd been paying attention.
Let's revamp the casting call
in the sky, see whose talent effloresces. That way
there'll be something to talk about next millennium.
The birds hear and drop to the grass.
Fireflies communicate spottily, but accurately.
The whole project is plain.
The rushes look good.
It was for this you spun your little web,
dear, and have somehow been rewarded. It is written

that only the unlikeliest take hold.
Tomorrow there will be fireworks, and then,
back to the chain of living and dying,
pleasing and ornery. The process shot whereby
scenery overcomes tedium, porch sitting.

Tonight we have tension and oneness,
arcane, arousing. Forgotten starlets
and minor nobility are apt to turn up in it.
And so he said not to go,
is standing stuttering there
fluffier than a dream in the park setting
where we were accustomed to dwell.

from *The New York Review of Books*

* * *

◇ ◇ ◇

The canals. The liquor coming through
the straw. The canals the land and
the bridge and the landing by the bridge
destroyed. The liquor. The little anger
growing inside the friends. The canal.
The pile of wood up against the bank.
The liquor. The friends. A little
anger growing inside them. The canal.
The jets. The wood in piles along
the bank. The dead. The jets. Liquor
through a straw. Speaking. A little anger
grows inside them. The jets. The dead.
The bank. The sky. The friends. The jets.
The dead. A little anger grows inside them.

from *Bird Dog*

Poseur

◊   ◊   ◊

I confess what I did in the tombs and the displays, and how I filtered the
    reports through an hourglass.
I admit to turning out the green light in the grapes.
I own up to emptying the squid of its ink.
All because I conceived of a rope with a noose at the end of it.
And I imagined an alchemical tide smothering the shore in gold.

I am not even the corpse at the end of this idea.
I tried to refill the night, but my eyes were open.
The two ends of the equator unraveled as I tried to cross.
The peeled apple took its skin back before I could eat.

Stars swept up their rays and the Milky Way poured itself over the rim of
    the planet rather than be named on my maps.
I awoke and was dead, so I decided to take my own life, and ended up
    alive after my self-inflicted demise.

from *The Iowa Review*

Ku(na)hay

◇ ◇ ◇

Form
Is One
Then Two Three

Content Is Another
Matter Altogether
No?

★

I Go Home
So Tired
Now

Slump
Into My
Slumber Once Again

Wake
To What
I Almost Forgot

★

No One Waits
Time Fails
Again

★

Still
The Quiet
Sucks Me Dry

A
Bone Solitary
Against the Wind

★

Trust No One
Gets You
Nowhere

from *Barrow Street*

Electrocuting an Elephant

◇ ◇ ◇

Like mourners, or men setting out early for a duel,
they follow these six tons, this hunk of flesh,
muddy and whorled, this elephant they tried once to hang
because she'd killed three men and survived

their carrots laced with cyanide. Coney Island, 1903,
and the handheld camera that gets all of this down
is a clock for seeing, as Barthes tells us it ought to be,
the image forever ticking over as three men,

in sepia and near-silhouette, step through a vacant lot,
follow the lead of the burly handler, who carries
a sleek whip, a coil of rope, as he leads his charge towards
the spot where they will set two of her feet

in copper shoes. Think of the boy, who sat in front of you
that year in school, led by the ear to the corner
of the classroom because he couldn't spell *vengeance*
after three turns. Think of the bull, three summers old,

pulled by the horns towards the place of sacrifice
so that bees might rise up out of its pooled blood.
And this too must be the way they took Bartholomew
after he made the King's brother deny *his* gods—

one guard gripping the prisoner's left arm and the three others,
who follow, unable to muster a single word
as they march down the main street of their village
towards the blue edge of the Caspian Sea,

where they will dispose of this son of Tolomai,
taking turns to open him with knives. What do they think
as they skulk after the condemned, this trinity,
who are not quite men yet despite their pristine uniforms,

or these others like extras from one of the first westerns
with their hats and moustaches, their say-nothing expressions
that barely make it beyond the ground sand of the lens
and onto this reel that unravels as I find myself

thinking again about that boy who, in *Scoil Muire*,
sat in the front row of those battered desks
with the defunct inkwells, the dry hinges that opened
into a box to store your books? This time he's reeling off

the names of birds. He makes a fist and hammers it
against his skull to bring forth robin redbreast, stonechat, crow,
while the rest of us raise our hands with what we think
are the right answers and hold our breaths trying hard not to laugh.

The truth is, I can't remember his name, only the way
his clothes reeked of stale milk and hay, and how
his father once tied a frying pan between the legs of their mongrel
to discourage it from running after cars. I'd like

to whisper this story into the ear of the keeper
before the film goes any further, before they reach
the spot where a crowd waits, impatient,
shifting from foot to foot. I'd like to tell him how,

after those four boys have done their dirty work
and turned into something older than they were before,
Bartholomew becomes that figure above the altar
in the Sistine Chapel who holds up a tanner's knife

and his own skin, another saint made patron
to those who wield the tools that worked his exit
from this world. And though it changes nothing,
I want to explain how, when the elephant falls, she falls

like a cropped elm. First the shudder, then the toppling
as the surge ripples through each nerve and vein,
and she drops in silence and a fit of steam to lie there
prone, one eye opened that I wish I could close.

from *Crazyhorse*

If See No End In Is

◇　◇　◇

What none knows is when, not if.
Now that your life nears its end
when you turn back what you see
is ruin. You think, It is a prison. No,
it is a vast resonating chamber in
which each thing you say or do is

new, but the same. *What none knows is
how to change.* Each plateau you reach, if
single, limited, only itself, in-
cludes traces of all the others, so that in the end
limitation frees you, there is no
end, if you once see what is there to see.

You cannot see what is there to see—
not when she whose love you failed is
standing next to you. Then, as if refusing the know-
ledge that life unseparated from her is death, as if
again scorning your refusals, she turns away. The end
achieved by the unappeased is burial within.

*Familiar spirit, within whose care I grew, within
whose disappointment I twist, may we at last see
by what necessity the double-bind is in the end
the figure for human life, why what we love is
precluded always by something else we love, as if
each no we speak is yes, each yes no.*

The prospect is mixed but elsewhere the forecast is no
better. The eyrie where you perch in
exhaustion has food and is out of the wind, if
cold. You feel old, young, old, young: you scan the sea
for movement, though the promise of sex or food is
the prospect that bewildered you to this end.

Something in you believes that it is not the end.
When you wake, sixth grade will start. The finite you know
you fear is infinite: even at eleven, what you love is
what you should not love, which endless bullies in-
tuit unerringly. The future will be different: you cannot see
the end. What none knows is when, not if.

from *Poetry*

Wanting Sumptuous Heavens

◇   ◇   ◇

No one grumbles among the oyster clans,
And lobsters play their bone guitars all summer.
Only we, with our opposable thumbs, want
Heaven to be, and God to come, again.
There is no end to our grumbling; we want
Comfortable earth and sumptuous Heaven.
But the heron standing on one leg in the bog
Drinks his dark rum all day, and is content.

from *The New Yorker*

Night Hunting

◇　◇　◇

Because we wanted things the way they were
in our minds' black eyes we waited. The beaver
raising ripples in a vee behind his head
the thing we wanted. A weed is what might grow
where you don't want it; a dahlia could be a weed,
or love, or other notions. The heart can't choose
to find itself enchanted; the hand can't choose
to change the shape of water. How strange, to hope
to see the signs of motion, to make an end
to Peter's old refrain: *He'll be along, son of a bitch,*
and then you best be ready. So sure, and so sure
that when he shines the light the thing will show
along the other shore. What next? Well,
you've killed animals before. Invited here
for company in the cold night, and because
ever handy with rifles. What next is wait
and see, what next may be the lone report, the ever-
widening circles, blood-blossom, the spirit rising slow
like oily smoke above still waters. We wanted
a pond to look like a pond: standing poplars,
shallows unsullied, fish and frogs and salamanders.
The gleaming back of fur and fat may not belong,
or may: God of varmints, God of will, forgive us
our trespasses. We know precisely what we do.

from *Ploughshares*

Jackson County
Public Library

Jackson Co PL - Medora Branch
(522-3412 http://MyJCLibrary.org/

John checked out:

1. **The complete poetry**, book by
Maya Angelou
Due: **Saturday, Apr 8, 2017**
Barcode: 39213000739999

2. **The best American poetry 2008,**
book by Charles Wright
Due: **Saturday, Apr 8, 2017**
Barcode: 39391060022899

You saved $46.00 by using the library!
MyJCLibrary ◙@MyJCLibrary

You were helped by Dawn

KSN-MED 2017-03-17 14:26

Entering

◇　◇　◇

Moonscape of snow at night.
To die, to crash,

could be a crush of snow.
All softness.

I imagine, driving alone,
being enveloped by snow, crashed into, quickly.

The mice must have these visions.
Talking quietly when they can't sleep

about tunneling in endless grain until, full of it,
completely enveloped by it, peacefully, it takes them.

from *Lyric*

Homage to Calvin Spotswood

◊　◊　◊

Yet not for those,
Nor what the potent victor in his rage
Can else inflict, do I repent or change,
Though changed in outward luster . . .
　　　　　　　—Paradise Lost, Bk. I

Because I couldn't bear to go back to the southside
of Richmond and the life I had led there—the blaring
televisions, the chained-up hounds, the cigarettes hissing
in ceramic saucers, the not never's, I'm fixin' to's,
the ain'ts—because anything at all was better than that,
I took the job. The four bucks an hour, the zip-front,
teal-colored, polyester uniform, the hairnets and latex gloves,
the intimate odors of piss and sweat, the eight hour
nighttime shifts of vomitus and shit, of death and death,
and then more death. Each day, I pinned on the badge that assigned me
to hell: nurse's aide in an oncology ward for terminal patients.

Calvin Spotswood was my first patient. His metal chart
proclaimed him: "Non-ambulatory, terminal C.A." A Goner,
the docs called him, a non-compliant asshole they wheeled
like a dying plant, out of the sun, out of the way,
so he could wither and perish at his own speed distant from those
with a happier prognosis.
They parked him in a dim back room so he could go unheard
when pain peeled him down to his disappearing center.

Calvin had dropped down through a chute in the day to day,
and skidded in for a landing on the flaming shores

of Stage III colo-rectal cancer. Nightly, he cooked there,
flipping back and forth on the grainy, cloroxed sheets
like a grilling fish. Timidly at first, I bathed the hot grate
of his ribs with tepid water, the cloth I dipped
almost sizzling dry on his heaving chest. I hated the feel
of his skin, the intimacy of my hands on his body. I hated
the smell beneath his sheets, the odor of his mouth. I hated
to touch him—a dying man, a devil, trapped, alive, in hell.

                                                    I feel
uncomfortable now, because he was black, imagining
Calvin as Milton's Satan, as if I am demonizing him unfairly,
or engaging in a stereotype based on race. But I had read the poem
and I recognized immediately the one who was "hurled headlong flaming"
from the gates of heaven, and "chained" for infinity "on the burning lake"
of his hospital bed. Like Lucifer, Calvin
was a troublingly complex antihero—a horrible person in many ways, stubborn
and stupid, had abused his nurses and cursed the doctors,
refusing the colostomy that might have prolonged—or saved—his life.
He wouldn't be unmanned, he said, shitting in a bag. No f-ing way.
He said "f-ing," instead of the full blown word,
a kind of delicacy I found peculiar, and then endearing.

And though the tumor, inexorably, day by day, shut him down, he wouldn't pray,
or console himself in any of the usual ways. Each afternoon,
he turned away from the Pentecostal preacher who stood with his Bible
at the foot of his bed, and said his name kindly and asked to say
a prayer or lay his hands upon the burning body. No f-ing way.

The tumor grew until it bound itself into his stomach wall.
Each move he made extracted a fiery arrow of flaming pain
from his rotten gut. And when the house staff figured
they had him beat, and organized a betting pool on how soon old Calvin
would entrust himself to the surgeon's knife so he could eat
again, he still declined, still whined for pussy, porno mags,
and chicken fried in bacon grease. A third year resident,
Harvard M.D., wrote an order for the supper Calvin thought
he craved: mashed potatoes and buttered bread, a chicken-battered,
deep-fried steak. Beaming, our man consumed it while his doctor lingered
outside his door to await the inevitable result of the natural process

of human digestion . . . Here is where I need to remind you that this
was back when the old U.Va. hospital still stood, on the brick-curbed rim
of Hospital Drive, where the sign saying Private really meant white, a reminder
of what passed for health care in the segregated South.
Nurses still wore bobby-pinned, absurd white hats that looked
as if they were about to levitate off of their heads.
The R.N.'s were white, the practicals, black.
And none of the docs, of course, were black.
But Calvin was, and the Civil Rights Act was a decade old,
so it was the New South, instead of the Old, where Calvin consumed
his last good meal, deluded into thinking a black man in the South
had finally won. An hour later, he knew he'd lost, and patients
two floors down could hear him screaming from the mouth
of the flaming crater he filled with curses.

Night after night, wrist deep in the tepid water I bathed him with,
I stood at his bedside and tried to change him from hot to cool
and listened to him discourse maniacally on the mysteries of gender:
Born again, he'd be a woman in slick red panties, a streetwalking
whore in high-heeled sandals and torn, black hose, opening his legs
for paper money, filling his purse with bucks to spend.
How anyone was granted a life like that he could never comprehend:
getting paid to fuck. His greatest treasure had been a dark red Pontiac with
      bucket seats
he'd drive to D.C.'s 14th Street to look for whores and a game of cards.
He'd been a lumberjack, he revealed one night. A quelling job,
and measured with his hands sphered into a circle, the muscles
jettisoned to illness. His strength had been his pride.
Now, he was a wiry and diminutive, sick stick of a man,
shriveled by a tumor. The image of his former power resided
in the two huge wives who guarded his door, one white, one black.
Passing between the corporeal portals of their womanly flesh,
my pale-toned puniness frightened me. But even in the final stages
of a violently invasive terminal carcinoma, nothing daunted Calvin—
not even the quarter ton of dominating, loud-mouthed women
with whom he had conceived six children. I marveled
at the unrancorous way they held each other, their cheap clothing
crinkling noisily, releasing that funky odor big people carry.
Their decalled fingernails, their huge, flopping breasts, their ornate hairdos—
the one teased up and lacquered high in place, the other cornrowed

flat with beads—their flamboyance so obvious I couldn't help
but apprehend what Calvin Spotswood thought was hot in women.
Not me, of course, skinny college girl with straight brown hair,
and wire rimmed glasses, dog-ear-ing Book I of *Paradise Lost*. . . .
What Calvin adored were the superfluous extras I tried to delete—
fat and loudness, clandestine odors of secreted musk.

At the end, cupping his withered, hairless testicles
in my cool, white palm because he asked me to, it wasn't anything
like witnessing a death. More like the birth of a new world, really,
he was entering alone. The little universe of sperm that twirled
beneath my hand, he was taking with him. On the burning bed,
his mouth lolled open in forgotten, wasted pleasure,
and I saw in my mind images of the South's strange fruit, the old photos
bound into books of black men who'd transgressed early in the century,
swinging heavily from trees—their demeaned postures and living deaths.
But Calvin was uncatalogued there. His name was written
in the dramatis personae of a slimmer text, an epic poem about the fall
from grace of a defiant, finger-flipping Beelzebub who dared
to challenge the creator of a world where black men swung
from the limbs of trees for admiring the backside of fair-skinned girls.
Calvin was the one kicking holes in the floor of that so called heaven to hasten
his eviction. And so I cupped his balls, I did, and stroked his dick, marveling,
at the force of life even at the end, and the inscrutability of a God
who would keep alive a man who claimed to hate his f ing guts
and nail into my mind forever, Calvin Spotswood in his final hours,
undiminished, unredeemed, unrepentant, his poor black body burning and
      burning.

from *storySouth*

Men

◊　◊　◊

There are also men in the world. Sometimes we forget, and think there are only women—endless hills and plains of unresisting women. We make little jokes and comfort each other and our lives pass quickly. But every now and then, it is true, a man rises unexpectedly in our midst like a pine tree, and looks savagely at us, and sends us hobbling away in great floods to hide in the caves and gullies until he is gone.

from *32 Poems*

Parallax

◇   ◇   ◇

Icicles plummet from the porch and sow
Drips, prisms, rainbows, daggers celestial
In their own right. They're lit with touch-and-go
Low beams. The moon slices residual
Storm clouds. Kaleidoscopes, the crystals crack
Colorless on the concrete and land in black.
You stare that black *more* black until the three
Branches across the street from a broken tree
Lose edges, shape, and still the vantage—last
Before you sleep. Through hedges you can see.
The train is coming slow and coming fast.

The later it gets, the more the sky will glow
In a strange reversal. Immaterial,
The stars are hidden in the indigo
Turning to rose, pinks so prophetical
Of sunny days—our nightly almanac.
And on the quarry lake the mallards quack.
Drakes lift and soar as if they're willowy
Feathers. A squawking goose attempts to flee
Their noise. He flaps his wings in the water's blast
Of droplets rising from the ice debris.
The train is coming slow and coming fast.

The more you sleep, the harder it is to throw
The nightmare off yourself, with its optical
Illusion and your eyes closed. Then, with no
Vision, your every where is visual.
I had a soundless dream once, saw the smack

Of cedar switches, saw the sting on black
Limp bodies, like spring blooms, hanged delicately
From a bough, strange fruit, decaying canopy
Of shade. I picked each one. One laughed at me.
He mouthed, blue-lipped, *We'll fall eventually.*
The train is coming slow. And coming fast,

The wind-blown icicles and jagged snow
Knock at my door, alive, no, visceral
As scraping fingernails, and the curio
Skyline moves like a shaken snow globe full
Of glittered flakes inside their hands. *We're back.*
Now let us in. The taps won't stop. I pack
My ears with tissue. *Yeah, those drapes could be*
Your noose. You're history. Yes, you. Go free—
But no—*sputter and snap. Look on, aghast.*
Go on, and gag on your own gravity—
The train is coming slow and coming fast:

What parallax (seesawing winks, the grow,
The shrink, the aweing always temporal,
The voices, mine). I see the train tracks show
Straight as a V. The lights bear destinal,
An oversight on dirt and the growing stack
Of branches. It seems they'll never shine where the track
Meets street and the land spreads constant, flat, a free
Expanse of time and space. Consistently
The horn blows louder, clearer, breezes gassed
With fumes when the red eyes start to flash. Fuck me.
The train is coming, slow and coming. Fast . . .

Swing low . . . the arm comes down. Illusory,
The scene melds quick as prose and poetry,
And I take it all in, still, as a metaphrast.
Pied Piper, play that piccolo; tell me
The train is coming slow and coming fast.

from *Sewanee Theological Review*

Handymen

◇　◇　◇

The furnace wheezes like a drenched lung.
You can't fix it.
The toilet babbles like a speed freak.
You can't fix it.
The fuse box is a nest of rattlers.
You can't fix it.
The screens yawn the bees through.
Your fingers are dumb against the hammer.
Your eyes can't tell plumb from plums.
The frost heaves against the doorjambs,
The ice turns the power lines to brittle candy.
No one told you about how things pop and fizzle,
No one schooled you in spare parts.
That's what the guy says but doesn't say
As he tosses his lingo at your apartment-dweller ears,
A bit bemused, a touch impatient,
After the spring melt has wrecked something, stopped something,
After the hard wind has lifted something away,
After the mystery has plugged the pipes,
That rattle coughs up something sinister,
An easy fix, but not for you.
It's different when you own it,
When it's yours, he says as the meter runs,
Then smiles like an adult.

from *The New Yorker*

Millay Goes Down

◇　◇　◇

What lips my lips have kissed, and where, and why?
And where? Yes, there. That summer in the barn,
he'd spread me on the hay bales, sixty-nine,
oblivious to scratches, clothes half-on,
we'd take forever. Salty, sweaty both,
and kissing back the taste, each other on
each other's avid lips. I learned a truth
perhaps more grown than I was then, so when
a lady I know says she won't do this,
that that's what whores are for, it makes me sad.
It seems a gift, devotion at the source
of all our humanness; best when, instead
of needing gesture, pressure, *Please, go south,*
he softly asks me, Do you want my mouth?

What lips my lips have kissed, and where, and why?
Why not's as good as why sometimes, why not
seduce this boy whose face, in candlelight,
looks slightly older, almost appropriate.
Your fingertips might almost brush his hand
as both of you dip bread into the oil.
You laugh and make it clear you understand
he'd rather hang out with a younger girl.
He says he's never had this wine, *mourvèdre;*
pronounces that he likes full-bodied, strong
and complicated wine (you think *educable,*
right on) and then his hand is on

your shoulder and he kisses you, his mouth
quite like a warm, *mourvèdre* fountain of youth.

from *Prairie Schooner*

Aubade in Autumn

◇   ◇   ◇

This morning, from under the floorboards
of the room in which I write,
Lawrence the handyman is singing the blues
in a soft falsetto as he works, the words
unclear, though surely one of them is *love*,
lugging its shadow of sadness into song.
I don't want to think about sadness;
there's never a lack of it.
I want to sit quietly for a while
and listen to my father making
a joyful sound unto his mirror
as he shaves—slap of razor
against the strop, the familiar rasp of his voice
singing his favorite hymn, but faint now,
coming from so far back in time:
Oh, come to the church in the wildwood . . .
my father, who had no faith, but loved
how the long, ascending syllable of *wild*
echoed from the walls in celebration
as the morning opened around him . . .
as now it opens around me, the light shifting
in the leaf-fall of the pear tree and across
the bedraggled back-yard roses
that I have been careless of
but brighten the air, nevertheless.
Who am I, if not one who listens
for words to stir from the silences they keep?
Love is the ground note; we cannot do
without it or the sorrow of its changes.

Come to the wildwood, love,
Oh, to the wiiildwood as the morning deepens,
and from a branch in the cedar tree a small bird
quickens his song into the blue reaches of heaven—
hey sweetie sweetie hey.

from *The New Yorker*

The Museum of Stones

◊　◊　◊

This is your museum of stones, assembled in matchbox and tin,
collected from roadside, culvert, and viaduct,
battlefield, threshing floor, basilica, abattoir,
stones loosened by tanks in the streets
of a city whose earliest map was drawn in ink on linen,
schoolyard stones in the hand of a corpse,
pebble from Apollinaire's *oui*,
stone of the mind within us
carried from one silence to another,
stone of cromlech and cairn, schist and shale, hornblende,
agate, marble, millstones, and ruins of choirs and shipyards,
chalk, marl, and mudstone from temples and tombs,
stone from the silvery grass near the scaffold,
stone from the tunnel lined with bones,
lava of the city's entombment,
chipped from lighthouse, cell wall, scriptorium,
paving stones from the hands of those who rose against the army,
stones where the bells had fallen, where the bridges were blown,
those that had flown through windows and weighted petitions,
feldspar, rose quartz, slate, blueschist, gneiss, and chert,
fragments of an abbey at dusk, sandstone toe
of a Buddha mortared at Bamiyan,
stone from the hill of three crosses and a crypt,
from a chimney where storks cried like human children,
stones newly fallen from stars, a stillness of stones, a heart,
altar and boundary stone, marker and vessel, first cast, lode, and hail,
bridge stones and others to pave and shut up with,
stone apple, stone basil, beech, berry, stone brake,
stone bramble, stone fern, lichen, liverwort, pippin, and root,

concretion of the body, as blind as cold as deaf,
all earth a quarry, all life a labor, stone-faced, stone-drunk
with hope that this assemblage of rubble taken together, would become
a shrine or holy place, an ossuary, immovable and sacred,
like the stone that marked the path of the sun as it entered the human dawn.

from *The New Yorker*

Rock Polisher

◇ ◇ ◇

Your father bought it, brought it
to the basement utility closet, waited
while a test pebble tumbled in it.
One week: he'd willed it to brilliance.
The grit kit's yours now, the silicon
carbide pack. Split it, have at it.
Jasper, agate, amethyst crystal,
it'll churn to a luster. Listen
to small rocks grind the big one down.
Stones in the driveway, pry them up, why not,
they'll fit, glass knobs on your mother's
bathroom cabinet, your baseball
and mitt, polish them, polish that
zero-win Peewee League season.
The thing your sister said and then
took back, you still have it, polish it,
polish the snowless Christmas
when all you'd hoped for was snow.
It's way past lights out now; you're crouched
above the barrel, feeding it
your school shoes, your haircut
in eighth grade—flat bangs
to the bridge of your nose—the moment
that girl on the track team touched
your wrist, then kept her fingers there,
the way you loved dumbly
and do. If the sun's up, it's nothing,
you're polishing, you're pouring in
the ocean rolling rocks into cobbles

too slowly, and the sky, it was
Mozart's, was Christ's sky,
no matter, dismantle it, drop it
into the tumbler, and you, too, get in there
with your dad and your mom and the cat,
one by one, the whole family,
and God's mercy, perfect at last.

from *New England Review*

In the Book
of the Disappearing Book

◊   ◊   ◊

It's a spring flowered dress that was her effacement.

On a train, and because of what windows do sometimes.
Her face is floating above the landscape
unaware.

I used to think that I was reporting my life to someone.
I was a radio.

I used to think things happening was unfolding.

The trees are blooming all through her
and there's no one to tell.

And the discipline of roads.
The icy discipline of to and from.

In the air of nothing, I used to think
I was understanding distance.

Green God, in your language of silences, tell me.

from *LIT*

Girl without
Her Nightgown

◊　◊　◊

The dance was slow, was slow, was slow.
Slow was the dance, very.
The dancer turned, her arms held out
As she came closer, slowly.

Wood grain steams in morning light, Mama,
The hulls of boats asunder.
Sterns still sport their stupid names.
The dance was slow, was slow, was slow.
Slow was the dance, very.

Scratch and snitch is the raven's game.
He nods and gossips.
Have you ever seen such happy rats?
What puppies.
The dance was slow, was slow, was slow.
Slow was the dance, very.

Those overturned boats are sepulchers of air.
All the boats that aren't washed up
Prowl the flooded streets, poke corpses with oars.
The water is on fire.
The dance was slow, was slow, was slow.
Slow was the dance, very.

Slow dance on the water, Mama.
I have a sack slung over my shoulder. Loot.
It's like I'm stealing my own soul.
The dance is slow, Mama.
I don't know where you are.

from *Verse*

Threshing

◊　◊　◊

The sky's light behind the mountain
though the sun is gone—this light
is like the sun's shadow, passing over the earth.

Before, when the sun was high,
you couldn't look at the sky or you'd go blind.
That time of day, the men don't work.
They lie in the shade, waiting, resting;
their undershirts are stained with sweat.

But under the trees it's cool,
like the flask of water that gets passed around.
A green awning's over their heads, blocking the sun.
No talk, just the leaves rustling in the heat,
the sound of the water moving from hand to hand.

This hour or two is the best time of day.
Not asleep, not awake, not drunk,
and the women far away
so that the day becomes suddenly calm, quiet, and expansive,
without the women's turbulence.

The men lie under their canopy, apart from the heat,
as though the work were done.
Beyond the fields, the river's soundless, motionless—
scum mottles the surface.

To a man, they know when the hour's gone.
The flask gets put away, the bread, if there's bread.

The leaves darken a little, the shadows change.
The sun's moving again, taking the men along,
regardless of their preferences.

Above the fields, the heat's fierce still, even in decline.
The machines stand where they were left,
patient, waiting for the men's return.

The sky's bright, but twilight is coming.
The wheat has to be threshed; many hours remain
before the work is finished.
And afterward, walking home through the fields,
dealing with the evening.

So much time best forgotten.
Tense, unable to sleep, the woman's soft body
always shifting closer—
That time in the woods: that was reality.
This is the dream.

from *The American Scholar*

Futures

◇   ◇   ◇

Midwinter. Dead of. I own you says my mind. Own what, own
                              whom. I look up. Own the looking at us
say the cuttlefish branchings, lichen-black, moist. Also
                              the seeing, which wants to feel more than it sees.
Also, in the glance, the feeling of owning, accordioning out and up,
                              seafanning,
& there is cloud on blue ground up there, & wind which the eye loves so deeply it
                              would spill itself out and liquify
                              to pay for it—
& the push of owning is thrilling, is spring before it
                              is—is that swelling—is the imagined fragrance as one
bends, before the thing is close enough—wide-
                              eyed leaning—although none of this can make you
                              happy—
because, looking up, the sky makes you hear it, you know why we have come it
                              blues, you know the trouble at the heart, blue, blue, what
pandemonium, blur of spears roots cries leaves master & slave, the crop destroyed,
                              water everywhere not
                              drinkable, & radioactive waste in it, & human bodily
waste, & what,
                              says the eye-thinking heart, is the last color seen, the last word
heard—someone left behind, then no behind—
                              is there a skin of the I own which can be scoured from inside the
                              glance—no,
                              cannot—& always
                              someone walking by whistling a
                              little tune, that's
life he says, smiling, there, that was life—& the heart branches with its

wild arteries—I own my self, I own my
leaving—the falcon watching from the tree—I shall torch the crop that no one else
have it whispers the air—
& someone's swinging from a rope, his rope—the eye
throbbing—day a noose looking for a neck—
the fire spidery but fast—& the idea of
friends, what was that, & the day, in winter, your lower back
started acting up again, & they pluck out the eyes at the end for
food, & don't forget
the meeting at 6, your child's teacher
wishes to speak to you
about his future, & if there is no food and the rain is everywhere switching-on as expected,
& you try to think of music and the blue of Giotto,
& if they have to eat the arms he will feel no pain at least, & there is a
sequence in which feeding takes
place—the body is owned by the hungry—one is waiting
one's turn—one wants to own one's
turn—and standing there,
don't do it now but you might remember kisses—how you kissed his arm in the sun
and
tasted the sun, & this is your
address now, your home address—& the strings are cut no one
looks up any longer
—or out—no—&
one day a swan appeared out of nowhere on the drying river,
it
was sick, but it floated, and the eye felt the pain of rising to take it in—I own you
said the old feeling, I want
to begin counting
again, I will count what is mine, it is moving quickly now, I will begin this
message "I"—I feel the
smile, put my hand up to be sure, yes on my lips—the yes—I touch it again, I
begin counting, I say *one* to the swan, *one*,
do not be angry with me o my god, I have begun the action of beauty again, on
the burning river I have started the catalogue,
your world,
I your speck tremble remembering money, its dry touch, sweet strange
smell, it's a long time, the smell of it like lily of the valley
sometimes, and pondwater, and how

                    one could bend down close to it
and drink.

from *London Review of Books*

I Am Your Waiter Tonight
and My Name Is Dmitri

◊   ◊   ◊

Is, more or less, the title of a poem by John Ashbery and has
No investment in the fact that you can get an adolescent
Of the human species to do almost anything,
Which is why they are tromping down a road in Fallujah
In combat gear and a hundred and fifteen degrees of heat
This morning and why a young woman is strapping
Twenty pounds of explosives to her mortal body in Jerusalem
Dulce et decorum est pro patria mori. Have I mentioned
That the other fact of human nature is that human beings
Will do anything they see someone else do and someone
Will do almost anything? There is probably a waiter
In this country so clueless he wears a t-shirt in the gym
That says Da Meat Tree. Not our protagonist. American amnesia
Is such that he may very well be the great-grandson
Of the elder Karamazov brother who fled to the Middle West
With his girl friend Grushenka—he never killed his father,
It isn't true that he killed his father—but his religion
Was that woman's honey-colored head, an ideal tangible
Enough to die for, and he lived for it: in Buffalo,
New York, or Sandusky, Ohio. He never learned much English,
But he slept beside her in the night until she was an old woman
Who still knew her way to the Russian pharmacist
In a Chicago suburb where she could buy sachets of the herbs
Of the Russian summer that her coarse white nightgown
Smelled of as he fell asleep, though he smoked Turkish cigarettes
And could hardly smell. Grushenka got two boys out of her body,
One was born in 1894, the other in 1896,

The elder having died in the mud at the Battle of the Somme
From a piece of shrapnel manufactured by Alfred Nobel.
Metal traveling at that speed works amazing transformations
On the tissues of the human intestine; the other son worked construction
The year his mother died. If they could have, they would have,
If not filled, half-filled her coffin with the petals
Of buckwheat flowers from which Crimean bees made the honey
Bought in the honey market in St. Petersburg (not far
From the place where Raskolnikov, himself an adolescent male,
Couldn't kill the old moneylender without killing her saintly sister,
But killed her nevertheless in a fit of guilt and reasoning
Which went something like this: since the world
Evidently consists in the ravenous pursuit of wealth
And power and in the exploitation and prostitution
Of women, except the wholly self-sacrificing ones
Who make you crazy with guilt, and since I am going
To be the world, I might as well take an axe to the head
Of this woman who symbolizes both usury and the guilt
The virtue and suffering of women induces in men,
And be done with it.). I frankly admit the syntax
Of that sentence, like the intestines slithering from the hands
Of the startled boys clutching their belly wounds
At the Somme, has escaped my grip. I step over it
Gingerly. Where were we? Not far from the honey-market,
Which is not far from the hay-market. It is important
To remember that the teeming cities of the nineteenth century
Were site central for horsewhipping. Humans had domesticated
The race of horses some ten centuries before, harnessed them,
Trained them, whipped them mercilessly for recalcitrance
In Vienna, Prague, Naples, London, and Chicago, according
To the novels of the period which may have been noticing this
For the first time or registering an actual statistical increase
In either human brutality or the insurrectionary impulse
In horses, which were fed hay, so there was, of course,
In every European city a hay-market like the one in which
Raskolnikov kissed the earth from a longing for salvation.
Grushenka, though Dostoyevsky made her, probably did not
Have much use for novels of ideas. Her younger son,
A master carpenter, eventually took a degree in engineering
From Bucknell University. He married an Irish girl

From Vermont who was descended from the gardener
Of Emily Dickinson, but that's another story. Their son
In Iwo Jima died. Gangrene. But he left behind, curled
In the body of the daughter of a Russian Jewish cigar-maker
From Minsk, the fetal curl of a being who became the lead dancer
In the Cleveland Ballet, radiant Tanya, who turned in
A bad knee sometime early 1971, just after her brother ate it
In Cao Dai Dien, for motherhood, which brings us
To our waiter, Dmitri, who, you will have noticed, is not in Baghdad.
He doesn't even want to be an actor. He has been offered
Roles in several major motion pictures and refused them
Because he is, in fact, under contract to John Ashbery
Who is a sane and humane man and has no intention
Of releasing him from the poem. You can get killed out there.
He is allowed to go home for his mother's birthday and she
Has described to him on the phone—a cell phone, he's
Walking down Christopher Street with such easy bearing
He could be St. Christopher bearing innocence across a river—
Having come across, inside an old envelope, a lock,
A feathery curl of his great-grandmother's Crimean-
Honey-bee-colored, Russian-spring-wildflower-sachet-
Scented hair in the attic, where it released for her
In the July heat and raftery midsummer dark the memory
Of an odor like life itself carried to her on the wind.
Here is your sea bass with a light lemon and caper sauce.
Here is your dish of raspberries and chocolate; notice
Their transfiguration of the colors of excrement and blood;
And here are the flecks of crystallized lavender that stipple it.

from *VOLT*

O my pa-pa

◇　◇　◇

Our fathers have formed a poetry workshop.
They sit in a circle of disappointment over our fastballs
and wives. We thought they didn't read our stuff,
whole anthologies of poems that begin, My father never,
or those that end, and he was silent as a carp,
or those with middles which, if you think
of the right side as a sketch, look like a paunch
of beer and worry, but secretly, with flashlights
in the woods, they've read every word and noticed
that our nine happy poems have balloons and sex
and giraffes inside, but not one dad waving hello
from the top of a hill at dusk. Theirs
is the revenge school of poetry, with titles like
"My Yellow Sheet Lad" and "Given Your Mother's Taste
for Vodka, I'm Pretty Sure You're Not Mine."
They're not trying to make the poems better
so much as sharper or louder, more like a fishhook
or electrocution, as a group
they overcome their individual senilities,
their complete distaste for language, how cloying
it is, how like tears it can be, and remember
every mention of their long hours at the office
or how tired they were when they came home,
when they were dragged through the door
by their shadows. I don't know why it's so hard
to write a simple and kind poem to my father, who worked,
not like a dog, dogs sleep most of the day in a ball
of wanting to chase something, but like a man, a man
with seven kids and a house to feed, whose absence

was his presence, his present, the Cheerios,
the PF Flyers, who taught me things about trees,
that they're the most intricate version of standing up,
who built a grandfather clock with me so I would know
that time is a constructed thing, a passing, ticking fancy.
A bomb. A bomb that'll go off soon for him, for me,
and I notice in our fathers' poems a reciprocal dwelling
on absence, that they wonder why we disappeared
as soon as we got our licenses, why we wanted
the rocket cars, as if running away from them
to kiss girls who looked like mirrors of our mothers
wasn't fast enough, and it turns out they did
start to say something, to form the words hey
or stay, but we'd turned into a door full of sun,
into the burning leave, and were gone
before it came to them that it was all right
to shout, that they should have knocked us down
with a hand on our shoulders, that they too are mystified
by the distance men need in their love.

from *Poetry* and *Poetry Daily*

Phone Booth

◇ ◇ ◇

There should be more nouns
For objects put to sleep
Against their will
The "booth" for instance
With coiled hidden wires
Lidded chrome drawers
Tipping up like lizards' eyes
We looked out into rhymed rain
We heard varying vowels
Rimbaud's vowels with colors
Orange or blue beeps
Types of ancient punctuation
The interpunct between words
A call became twenty-five cents
Times in a marriage we went there
To complain or flirt
A few decades and we wised up
Got used to the shadow
The phone booth as reliquary
An arm could rest
On the triangular shelf
A briefcase between the feet
A pen poked into acoustic holes
While we gathered our actions/wits
For magic and pain
The destiny twins
Some of us scratched pale glyphs
Onto the glass door while talking

One day we started to race past
And others started racing
Holding phones to their ears
Holding a personal string
To their lips
If there are overages
There might be nouns for
The clotting of numbers in the sky
So thick the stars can't shine through
A word for backing away
From those who shout to their strings
In the airport while eating
We loved the half-booths
Could cup one hand on the mouthpiece
Lean two-thirds out to talk to a friend
Sitting in the lobby
The universe grows
We are dizzy as mercury
We are solitudes aided by awe
Let us mourn secrets told to
Fake wood and the trapezoidal seat
Perfume in the mouthpiece
Like a little Grecian sash
Why did we live so fast
The booth hid our ankles
We twisted the rigid cord
As we spoke
It made a kind of whorl

from *The New Yorker*

49

Muchness

◊   ◊   ◊

I saw you in the rainy morning
from the window of the hotel room,
running down the gangplank to board the boat.

You were wearing your famous orange pants,
which are really apricot
and the boat rocked a little
as you stepped on its edge.

You were going to work
with your backpack and sketchbook
and your bushy gray hair
which bursts out in weather
like a steel wool bouquet.

That's how my heart is, I thought—
It lies coiled up inside of me, asleep,
then springs out and shocks me
with all of its muchness.

But as I was dreaming, your boat pulled away.
Then there was just the gray sheen
of the harbor left behind, like unpolished steel
and the steep green woods that grow down to the shore,
and the gauze of mist on the hills.

It was your vanished boat
which gave the scene a shape,
with its suggestion of journey and destination.

And the narrative then, having done its work,
it vanished too,
leaving just its affectionate cousin description behind;

—Description,
which lingers,
and loves for no reason.

from *Poetry*

Cane Fire

◇   ◇   ◇

At the bend of the highway just past the beachside melon and papaya stands
Past the gated entrance to the Kuilima Hotel on the point where Kubota once
                                            loved to fish,
The canefields suddenly begin—a soft green ocean of tall grasses
And waves of wind rolling through them all the way to the Ko'olau,
                    a velvet green curtain of basalt cliffs covered in mosses.
Tanaka Store comes up then, *makai* side of the highway, *towards the sea,*
And, whatever it looks like now—curio conchs dangling from its porch rafters
Festooned with birdcages of painted bamboo, wooden wafers of old shave-ice
                                            cones and prices—
I think of stories and photos from nearly a century ago
When Gang No. 7 worked *hoe-hana* and *happai-ko* out near here,
Bending to weed the hoe rows or shouldering a 30# bundle of sticky cane,
Trying not to think of the fresh tubs of cold *tofu* lying on the wet plank floors
                                            in its grocery aisles
Or the money they owed for bags of rice, cans of Crisco, and *moxa* pellets
They used for flaming the skin on their backs at night, relieving aches with
                                            flashes of pain,
Remembering fire was for loneliness, smoke was for sorrow.

And, if I see a puffer fish, dried and lacquered, full of spikes and pride,
Suspended over a woodframe doorway as I glance back while driving by,
Or if the tall, television actor with long blonde hair and a cowboy's gait
Walks from the parking lot toward the picnic tables of the decrepit shrimp shack
Where the old icehouse used to be, where the cameras and film crew now stand,
I'm not going to lean forward into wanting or desire, amusements of my time,
But remember instead that Pine Boy died here one afternoon in 1925.

I know this because I count from the year my grandmother was born in 1910,
The year Twain died and the comet passed close to them sitting among the cane at night,
A pearly fireball and long trail of alabaster light over the empty Hawaiian sea,
And forward to the story of how she was fifteen when the *lunas* called her to calm him.

Matsuo was her adopted brother, a foundling of Hawaiian blood raised Shigemitsu
And sent, at sixteen, to work the canefields with his brothers and uncles.
No incidents until the day the field bosses ordered cane fires to be lit,
Workers oiling the roots and grass, torchers coming through to light the cane,
Burn its leaves down to harvestable stalks that could be cut and stacked.

Something flamed in Matsuo too, because he grabbed a *luna* and cut his throat,
Ran into the blazing fields, and could be heard whimpering *jul'like one pig*,
His cries coming through the rising smoke and crackle of the cane fires.

What words he said I've never been told—only that he moved within the fields,
Staying ahead or within the fire, and could not be coaxed out
                              or pursued with dogs or on a horse.

Among the Gang, there was no one who doubted his own death
                              should they follow him.
But Tsuruko, his sister, was called, *tita* who had nursed with him,
Rushed out of school and brought in the manager's car out to the fields,
The man opening the door and taking her hand *as if she haole wahine ladat!*
As she stepped from the cab and onto the scorched plantation earth.

The image I have is of her walking over opened ground absolutely cleared of cane,
The brown and black earth mounded up around her as she stood among small hillocks
                              as if a score of graves had just been dug,
The soft, inconstant breezes pressing a thin cotton dress against her skin,
Her back to the crowd while she says something into the wind that only the cane
                              and Matsuo could hear.

And then his crying ceased and he emerged magically from a curtain of smoke and cane,
His eyes tarred and patched with burnt oil and charcoaled with molasses.
He stood out for an instant, in front of wicking flames,
Then felt the bead of a rifle on him, and he slipped quickly back in,
The cane fires muffling whatever words he might have called as they took him.

The crouching lion of a lava bluff juts near the road,
And I know the jeep trail will come up next,
A cattle fence and white and brown military sign its marker.
It's where the radar station is, far past the fields and up-mountain
Where the sluice-waters start and the apples blossom,
Leaving white popcorn flowers dappling the mud with faint,
                              perishable relicts of rage and beauty.

from *Ploughshares*

The Rape of the Daughters of Leucippus by Castor and Pollux

◊   ◊   ◊

—Peter Paul Rubens, 1619

For ages, all of us have had the story wrong,
    and it is probably Pure Folly
to imagine that the time-honored (or time-*shamed*)
    version of this indecorously
illustrious and so often illustrated
    episode can be altered so late
in the day; but Rubens's vision of Truth prevails,
    and misconstruction must give way!
First of all, as far back as Homer we were told
    the name *Dioscuri* (sons of Zeus)
bestowed *late in the day* on Castor & Pollux
    is actually a misnomer:

Castor, whom Leda, in her more conjugal moods,
    liked to say was the Spitting Image
of Tyndareos, the "cuckold king of Sparta"
    (*everyone knew*)—Castor was, of course,
merely a mortal, but Pollux, his so-called "twin,"
    somehow managed to Figure It Out,
i.e., divined he must be more or less divine
    thanks to the Swan-rape (*everyone knew*),
and never let Leda forget What Had Happened,

hard as the poor deluded dear tried
not to prefer godly traits to human ones, when
she managed to recognize them.

Once smitten, twice shy, was her odd excuse, adding
with a little laugh: *Whatever shape*
Fate determines to show . . . I doubt she even knew
for sure which of her boys was "special,"
and Pollux would never have let her get wind of
the hard-and-fast bargain he'd driven
with his fast-and-loose Begetter, ensuring that
on alternate days the *twin heroes*
would share a single immortality, half on
Olympus and half among the Shades,
though their earthly life would be simultaneous—
a complicity of *marauders!* . . . *

         *Cleaving to Castor, Pollux deplored the after-
            effects of the Swan's exploits; himself
         hatched rather than born (those god-awful gaudy shells,
            not bronzed babybooty but gilded
         —*Leda insisted*—"for sentimental reasons";
            and since displayed through countless aeons
         to travelers like gullible Pausanias
            touring the Historic Sites of Greece),
         while his "false twin," the utterly mortal sibling,
            was compelled, from first breath to last gasp,
         to confront the Usual Facts of human birth
            and consequently of human death.

Barely adolescent, the boys manifested
    shameless and fully *shared* hankerings
for violent sexual conquest, beyond doubt
    inherited, honed to mastery
on one another (the mortal prince most often
    took for himself the ravisher's role—
was this, too, a "usual fact"? or merely
    a minimally invasive act:
as far as a god's body might be manhandled?).

Now, though, at man's estate, both preferred
virgin girls in pairs, taken turn and turn about
    in consummated emulation . . .

How the plains of Sparta echoed to maiden plaints!
    (although not always in demurral),
latterly to those of Leucippus's two daughters,
    Hilaera and Phoebe, long betrothed
to Lynceus and Idas, brothers burning now
    to requite the rape of their brides
on the very morning they were to be married.
    In pitched battle, Castor and the two
expectant bridegrooms would perish
    after the classic violations
in an equally classic revenge, whereupon
    Pollux could deliver his brother,

as Zeus had promised, to an immortality
    every other day. And meanwhile
in another part of the Spartan wilderness,
    Rubens had set (and cleared away)
the scene which led to such funest consequences,
    as well as to the corrigendum
I hereby undertake: *The Rape of the Daughters
    of Leucippus* is not what is here.
Look again, look closer. Those hysterical girls
    are not being, they have already
been raped—they are *being dumped:* Phoebe delivered
    by Castor (in armor and gold chains)

to the ground; Hilaera already there, still braced
    on the knee of naked Pollux, done
with her but still helpful, before leaving to fight
    angry bridegrooms, angrier fathers
altogether elsewhere. Here, the sisters will lie
    in each other's arms a while, shed
a few tears, and then collect their golden rags
    and begin, not talking much, the long
trudge somewhere out of the picture. Ask Leda:

memory takes some time to compose
itself into a story all of us want to believe,
although of course it wasn't like that.

from *Five Points*

Snoring

◇　◇　◇

There's an explanation for everything, even the need to explain.
Take, for example, the summer I lived with my father in an old folks home.
He had a new job, running the place, and we lived in a room,
My mother 300 miles away trying to sell our house.
I was nineteen and learned on the first night what a powerful snorer he was
And also how well she'd trained him. Eventually I thought I'd discovered
Their spiritual bond or that I'd unlocked a spiritual power.
All eventually explained away by a friend. But let me testify first
To my dawning awareness that either the mind and its intangible reach
Or an energy greater than anything so material had entered me—
Entered and extended from me. I thought I'd found
The bond between my parents, or one strand of it, one element of the glue,
Which even then, that summer, was breaking down, unstable after years of stability.
He snored, his motor chuff, dog honk and blare woke me, and I rose,
Went to his bed across the room, shook him and said, "You're snoring!"
It wasn't like Samuel shaking Eli awake, asking, "Did you call me?" But one night
I learned that throwing my legs out of bed would silence him. A snort and a sigh
And he was mute. The room closed its lids to the rich dark of slumber.
It took the whole summer but I discovered what years of bed fellowship had taught
    him.
And one night, waking to his thundering rumble, I simply thought, "Stop." He
    stopped.

That summer we drove home to Mother on weekends, talking theology. He told me
His theory of heaven, or rather what happened, he thought, when we died,
For there was a good deal of dying that summer, it being one of the pastimes
    at the other home.
His theory was based on First John Chapter Four Verse Eight. He that loveth not,
    knoweth not God,

For God is love. At death, he believed, Love greets us and depending
On our knowledge of love, we either return the greeting or find ourselves at a loss.

Years later, after I told him this story of my parents' former harmony,
And how that summer my father and I had roomed together, and, I should add,
How I worked all day on the home's maintenance crew,
Painting the recently vacated rooms and moving death-beds into storage,
The friend I told my story to explained that a simple change of breathing in the room I
    shared with my father
Would have signaled him to stop. I thought I had moved in the spirit,
With a spirit body and its lithe array of senses, limber knowledge-gatherers,
Kinetic fliers like and unlike thought, like but faster than light, that wondrousness.
I had lain in the dark amazed that I could affect someone with a thought.
Only to have this wonder explained away quite sensibly, yes, it had to be true, quite
    rationally.
And besides my parents' spiritual bond had long been broken, without my help or
    hindrance.

And as for heaven, what of those who never loved because they were never loved,
The loveless and unlovable, in who knows what state of snoring-repellent life?
When they die, either they find the arousal, the constant arousal of love,
Glaring them in the face, shaking them with its welcome, and do not understand.
Or they find another welcome, the rich dark of slumber, which passes all
    understanding.

from *The American Poetry Review*

GEORGE KALAMARAS

Francis Ponge Is on Fire

◊   ◊   ◊

The match is on fire. No, the priest is on fire. No, Francis Ponge is on fire. Fire gives Ponge his body, gives his silk oyster-cream self brilliance. It is a body alive with eclectic thought, with ocean current. The emanating sparrow secretions from his left ear give his body light. It is dark blood-light, like the moment of birth someone who is dying remembers.

The priest is on fire. His black robes are charred parts of Ponge's heart baptizing this child and that. Someone has eased a starter pistol into the rib, Francis Ponge's rib. Someone says, *Stick 'em up! Drop the baptismal fountain! Give me your oyster!* It is not unlike the confusion of a night of unrequited sex. *Give me your oyster* is rebutted with the sweaty sheet-tangle of, *No, give me* **your** *oyster.*

The university is on fire. The papers are plentiful stars that are, for once, not snobby but in their fragility are about to be human. The brilliant books are alive with wanton ocean depth, burning flood lamps that dim as they enter the mouths of sharks. It is a depth Francis Ponge seeks in the match extinguished in the oyster's rubber limb, an almost holy singe he exacts with the desperate flicking of a pick each evening between each tooth for the charred star and its scar.

from *Sentence*

Recuperation from the Dead Love through Christ and Isaac Babel

◊　◊　◊

If you spend all night reading Babel and wake on an island
　　metropolis on your raft bed under a patent-leather sky
　　　　with the stars pecked out, you may not sense
the presence of Christ, the Red Cavalry having hacked up
　　all those Poles, the soldiers hugging each other
　　　　with their hatchets. This morning, my ex-man
is a caved-in box of disposable razors to ship back.
　　He wore a white Y on his baseball cap. Night
　　　　was a waterfall down his face.
Marry me meant *You're a life-support system*
　　for a nice piece of ass, meant *Rent*
　　　　this space. Leaving the post office, I enter
the sidewalk's gauntlet of elbows. All around me,
　　a locust buzz as from the book of Job. Yet I pray, I
　　　　pray: Christ my Lord, my savior,
and my good brother, sprinkle me
　　with the blood of the lamb. Which words
　　　　make manifest his buoyancy in me.
If the face of every random pedestrian is prayed for,
　　then the toddler in its black pram
　　　　gnawing a green apple can become Baby Jesus.
And the swaggering guy in a do-rag idly tossing an orange
　　into the crosswalk's air might feel Heaven's winds
　　　　suck it from his grasp as offering.

Maybe the prospect of loss—that potential emptiness
    granted his hands—lets him grin so wide at me.
        His gold teeth are a sunburst.
When the scabby man festooned with purple rags
    shoulders an invisible rifle to shoot him, he pirouettes,
        clutching his chest. Light applause follows
his stagger to the curb. The assassin bows.
    These are my lords, my saviors, and my good brothers.
        Plus the Jew Isaac Babel, who served the Red Calvary,
yet died from a bullet his own comrade chambered.
    That small hole in his skull
        is the pit on the map we sailed from.

from *The New Yorker*

Though He Tarry

◊   ◊   ◊

I believe with perfect faith in
the coming of the Messiah
and though he tarry I will
wait daily for his coming
said Maimonides in 1190
or so and 44 percent
of people polled in the USA
in 2007 are also waiting
for him to show up in person—
though of course he won't <u>be</u> a person.

Do we want to save our planet,
the only one we know of,
so the faithful 44 percent
can be in a state of high alert
in case he arrives in person
though of course he won't <u>be</u> a person?

According to Stephen Jay Gould
    science and religion are
    non-overlapping magisteria.
    See each elbowing the other
    to shove over on the bed
    they're condemned to share?
    See how they despise, shrink back
    from accidental touching?
It's no surprise that
60 percent of scientists
say they are nonbelievers.

But whether you're churchy or not
what about the planet?
Damn all of you with dumpsters.
Damn all who do not compost.
Damn all who tie their dogs out
on bare ground, without water.
Damn all who debeak chickens
and all who eat them, damn
CEOs with bonuses,
corporate jets, trophy wives.

Damn venal human nature
lurching our way to a sorry
and probably fiery finale. . . .
If only he'd strap his angel wings on
in the ether and get his licensed
and guaranteed ass down here—
though of course he won't <u>be</u> a person—
if only he wouldn't tarry.

from *The Hudson Review*

Skull Trees, South Sudan

◊ ◊ ◊

Arok, hiding from the Arabs in the branches of a tree,
two weeks surviving on leaves,
legs numb, mouth dry.
When the mosquitoes swarmed
and the bodies settled limp as petals under the trees,
he shinnied down, scooping out a mud pit with his hands
sliding into it like a snake,
his whole body covered except his mouth.
Perhaps others were near him,
lying in gloves of mud, sucking bits of air through the swamp holes,
mosquitoes biting their lips,
but he dared not look.

What did he know of the rest of South Sudan, pockmarked with bombs,
skull trees with their necklaces of bones,
packs of bony Lost Boys
roving like hyenas towards Ethiopia,
tongues, big as toads, swelling in their mouths,

the sky pouring its relentless bombs of fire. Of course they were
tempted to lie down for a moment,

under the lone tree, with its barely shade,
to rest just a little while before moving on,

the days passing slyly, hallucinations
floating like kites above them

until the blanched bones lay scattered in a ring around the tree,
tiny ribs, skulls, hip bones—a tea set overturned,
as the hot winds whistled through them
as they would anything, really,

and the sky, finally exhausted,
moving on.

from *The Kenyon Review*

From *"Hallelujah Blackout"*

◇   ◇   ◇

On the shore's river-pitted ruins
             Where no one can be

Beautiful   Suckholes & stones   So beautiful

        Below the citybright
                  & everywhere exhaust

As steel-heavy sheets whiten the banks with rain

        Until above the bridge   The tremulous   Wrenching

Away of clouds   & over the water flashes
        The rivet-split sky   Bursting iron-lunged

                  & orange

                  ~

In that symphony of firework

             I am forever listening
             To the sky breaking ribs

        Until darkness falls   With fingers buried in light
                  Sockets   & holes

from *AGNI*

Of Love and Other Disasters

◊　◊　◊

The punch-press operator from Flint
met the assembler from West Virginia
in a bar near the stadium. Neither
had anything in mind, so they conversed
about the upcoming baseball season
about which neither cared. We could
be a couple, he thought, but she was
all wrong, way too skinny. For years
he'd had an image of the way a woman
should look, and it wasn't her, it wasn't
anyone he'd ever known, certainly not
his ex-wife, who'd moved back south
to live with her high-school sweetheart.
About killed him. I don't need that shit,
he almost said aloud, and then realized
she'd been talking to someone, maybe
to him, about how she couldn't get
her hands right, how the grease ate
so deeply into her skin it became
a part of her, and she put her hand,
palm up, on the bar and pointed
with her cigarette at the deep lines
the work had carved. "The life line,"
he said, "which one is that?" "None,"
she said, and he noticed that her eyes
were hazel flecked with tiny spots
of gold, and then—embarrassed—looked
back at her hand, which seemed tiny
and delicate, the fingers yellowed

with calluses but slender and fine.
She took a paper napkin off the bar,
spit on it and told him to hold still
while she carefully lifted his glasses
up on his forehead, leaving him half
blind, and wiped something off
above his left cheekbone. "There,"
she said, lowering his glasses, "I
got it," and even with his glasses on
what she showed him was nothing
he could see. He thought, better
get out of here before it's too late, but
knew too late was what he wanted.

from *The New Yorker*

J . D .   M c C L A T C H Y

Resignation

◇   ◇   ◇

I like trees because they seem more resigned to
the way they have to live than other things do.
　　　　　　　　　—Willa Cather

Here the oak and silver-breasted birches
Stand in their sweet familiarity
While underground, as in a black mirror,
They have concealed their tangled grievances,
Identical to the branching calm above
But there ensnared, each with the others' hold
On what gives life to which is brutal enough.
Still, in the air, none tries to keep company
Or change its fortune. They seem to lean
On the light, unconcerned with what the world
Makes of their decencies, and will not show
A jealous purchase on their length of days.
To never having been loved as they wanted
Or deserved, to anyone's sudden infatuation
Gouged into their sides, to all they are forced
To shelter and to hide, they have resigned themselves.

from *The New Yorker*

The Last Wolf
in Edmonson County

◊   ◊   ◊

Then I stood below the pedestal of Dismal Rock
as shadows straggled up like sheep from the river.
I wanted to believe his ghost might prowl among them,
that something of his hunger might still be limping
down a faint scent trail to its end, but I could not.
Autumn lit the wicks of the leaves; the river, foaming,
garbled, recovered its voice. I did not climb
the flash-lit, switchback trail to the rockhouse.
I did not stand before the petroglyphs again
nor rake at the midden of ash below them with a stick.
I waited until the dark took everything
but the sound of water: the spillway's troughs of stone,
the dam's thick plug. I waited where the blood spoor
of local narrative intersects a trail gone cold,
and what came stalking there was not a shade, though
it moved with stealth among the sawbriars, lit by nothing.

from *Poetry*

W. S. MERWIN

A Letter to Su Tung P'o

◇   ◇   ◇

Almost a thousand years later
I am asking the same questions
you did the ones you kept finding
yourself returning to as though
nothing had changed except the tone
of their echo growing deeper
and what you knew of the coming
of age before you had grown old
I do not know any more now
than you did then about what you
were asking as I sit at night
above the hushed valley thinking
of you on your river that one
bright sheet of moonlight in the dream
of the water birds and I hear
the silence after your questions
how old are the questions tonight

from *The New Yorker*

Ritual

◇   ◇   ◇

as one who casts the word *bread* upon the word *waters,* testing

as one who not believing something will rise up from
those waters, but not disbelieving either
casts out her voice

as one curious or hungry or filled with longing breaks
off just the crust of a word, throwing
the way she threw as a girl when everyone

told her that was not the way
to throw and expecting little or nothing
looks into the blackness   but the waves

are not black they will be deep
scummed violet and bronze
like a memorial forgotten
                              would it have made a difference
if she had cast the word *thread* upon those waters
unspooling what she spoke   sewing

knots and tangles into waves and might
thread return to her as *dread* or even *dead*

as one who does not know what it is she wants
but wants her wanting sanctified
and anointed with myrrh and futility   black

the waves are black and laced with white
shrouds which pass
                    into nothingness and the way
a snowflake vanishes
into the waves her voice cast out from her

she has wanted so long such a lifetime not
knowing what it is she wants

as one who has eaten joy for no good reason
with no idea where it came from
and wept in her sleep forgetting afterward who

embraced her but the next day feeling the loss
as one who casts word after word
into nothingness fillets ruins of foam cresting

so the word *lover* vanishes into water
and with it go *fervor* and *savior forever*
and *elixir*
                as one who keeps opening and closing
so the word *birth* is buried in *earth* so
the word *breath* is lost in *death*

as one who waits to see the eyes of water
roll back into depth, who waits
to see the depth rolled back and parted so she

can fly through and thinks she sees wings
and knows herself deluded
even though she sees
                as one who marked off
her wanting who staked its boundaries and let
nothing cross over to staunch or squander it

as one who says I want therefore I am

as one who saw the word *bread* float in the word *water*
before they both sank under
the weight of her wanting

as one who thought she saw something leap
but it may have been the word *motion* coming back
to her shadow for shadow

what is the hunger to know the other's
hunger built up like an altar

sacrifice she understood the blood
of her hunger wanting hunger for hunger, its
teeth in her flesh the word *flesh* the word *hunger*

as one who the more she looked saw less
what little there was she messed into more mess
there was no depiction in it

what would it take to register the quickness
the alacrity to blow out

the candle of the waves the word *candle*

the voice of the waves the word *voice*

the living face of the promise of the voice

from *The American Poetry Review*

The Water Cooler

◇　◇　◇

They're poisoning the atmosphere
now you and I've split
because they're trying to get something clear.
The mistletoe puts up its mitts

now you and I've split.
The black oaks jostle
and the mistletoe puts up its mitts
to vie for the sweet-throated throstle

where the black oaks jostle
over a back fence
and vie for the sweet-throated throstle,
seeming no less tense

over a back fence
than the chestnuts dishing the dirt,
seeming no less tense
than so many introverts,

than the chestnuts dishing the dirt
down by the water cooler.
Like so many introverts,
like all the other carpoolers

down by the water cooler,
they cough up their lungs.
Like all those other carpoolers,
the maples wag their tongues

and cough up their lungs
because they're trying to get something clear.
The maples wag their tongues.
They're poisoning the atmosphere.

from *The New Yorker*

The Gate of Abraham

◇   ◇   ◇

*Brother Yves caught sight of an old woman with a bowl full
of flaming coals and a flask filled with water. "What are
you going to do with those," he asked. She answered that
with the fire she intended to burn up paradise and destroy
it, and with the water she would quench the fires of
hell . . .*

—Joinville, Chronicle of the Crusades

1

In the first weeks of that endless skirmish
the king was stranded in the sea-lanes at Damietta.
The sultan was garrotted by his own guard.
Mercenaries melted away, nuncios
took to the high seas in a leaky skiff.
I was remanded to Acre with the clerics
to grow old among jongleurs and goliards.
My life seemed huge, like a cloak too big,
after the narrow moment of killing.

At Michaelmas a knight with a suppurating wound
begged extreme unction and I confessed him.
I blessed him with two fingers, *ego te absolvo.*
His eyes rolled back, he coughed and stiffened,
but I could not remember a word of his sins.
My mind was humming with my own failure.

Perhaps I had escaped the bitterness of victory
for an intimate defeat, riddled with waiting.

2

In winter, the camp teemed with refugees,
spies, corrupted saints, rival chroniclers,
though nothing happened in Outremer
except doves volleying through dusty cedar
in pursuit of their bruised voices
and a cricket temporizing inside a wall.

Evenings I longed for the lisp of Poitiers,
the sarcasm of the Angevin back country.
Once, wandering from barracks to barracks,
I met a toothless woman in the blue wimple
of Perigord, stumbling with a bowl and gourd.

I begged for a sip, and to warm my hands.
She agreed, but counted to herself,
staring at my Adam's apple. I dawdled
just for her company. She smelled of old age,
stale Burgundy, the thyme of my village.

But she was in no mood for delay.
She pried my fingers from her hem,
picked up her burdens, and limped
towards the Gate of Abraham.

I warned her, that way is the desert.
Nothing there except stones and wind,
the mountains of the holy land like frayed silk.
Once you enter those names—Hebron, Moriah—
you will find only scripture, no hearth,
just darkness and the radiant sheen of ink.

She kept going. I watched until sundown,
when the glint of the coals began to waver.

From across that dry river the enemy prayer
rose, searing in its desire for God,
the opposing echoes, the renegade dogs,
and at last the opposing stillness, deepening
as her steps receded.

from *Barrow Street*

Every Night

◊   ◊   ◊

Federal holding cell, Hughes County Jail

Fights. Never quiet—like years back
with the folks, but ratcheted-up, bloodied,
multiplied, till the badge writes the last two
shovers up, says he'll do the same for all of us
if we can't keep the crybabies smothered
I WANT SOME PEACE,
SLEEP, NO MORE GETTING
OUT OF THE CHAIR, IT'S BAD ENOUGH
WATCHING YOU IDIOTS ON
THE MONITOR, NEXT TIME I'LL SHUT
THE TV OFF IN HERE FOR YOU,
GIVE YOU A REASON TO COMPLAIN

—do that. Myron's flat voice from under
his blanket above me, only sound from up
there in two days except his creaking down
for hotdog-chow or a crap—only guy no one
yells at when he's on the shitcan—what a
display, someone every hour stinking this cage
of sixteen waiting to be shipped, strung out,
on top of each other every minute—bunk,
shower, shitter, picnic table, TV remote to
fight over, that's it. I thought machinery'd
ruined my ears already, but 24-7 banging and
shouting has them way more gone. Maybe
Myron's working on hearing nothing. Finally
weather over 75, so they were herding us out

thirty minutes a day to watch a 20 × 20 patch
of sky framed by concertina, till one guy's pal
tossed a pack of Pall Malls over and that was it
for light and air—*leave the cigs alone*, Myron
growled. Stupid joes got us all shaken down.

Now tonight they throw in a fish, kidnapped
his own kid or something *HOW
CAN THEY TAKE HER* slamming
his arms at the bars till they're bleeding,
then old Buffalo yelling *AIDS! GIT 'IM
OUTA HERE*—hammers his own fists
on the steel for the hack to come, clank in,
lock the TV off, and turn his back on
two bulldogs in the corner working
the fresh guy over—*SHE'S MY KID,
FOR GOD'S SAKE—FORGET GOD
DIPSHIT, YOU'RE IN NOW, YOU'RE
A GONER* and Buffalo cranking the shower
*STOP THE BLOOD, THROW 'IM IN
THE SLIME, I TELL YA, KEEP
'IM AWAY FROM ME*
till Fuzzy pulls a shank and shuts him up.

Myron groans, rolls over, whacked-out Scott
snores on, *peace, sleep, chair,* the turnkey's
words echo long after his last shudder of the bars
—it's all I wanted too, to find the stuff that would
take me out—*peace, sleep, chair,* close as it gets
to lullaby in here, close as any of us ever
got maybe—TV black, our own soundtrack
jagging and vibrating till god knows when.

from *Ploughshares*

The Window at Arles

◊   ◊   ◊

Even the moon set him going, with its blank stare;
even the walls of the café, which seemed to tilt
and sway as he watched them, green with absinthe.
"It is a wonderful thing to draw a human being."
All night, Van Gogh painted, and then scraped paint from the easel;
the stiff sound of palette knife on canvas,
scratching, made him think of a hungry animal.
Women came and posed.
"It is a wonderful thing to paint a human being, something
that lives," he told Théo; "it is confoundedly difficult,
but after all it is splendid."
When the money for models ran out,
he bought plaster casts of hands and hung them
from the crossbeams of his room,
and woke to the sound of their knocking in the wind.

★

One night Van Gogh sat in a chair, staring.
Brush in one hand, milk saucer in the other.
The tea was weak. Nothing came. In the morning,
one of his models brought bread and cheese
and made him eat. That afternoon,
he broke the plaster casts, banging hand into hand
until he stood in a storm of dust, coughing.

★

When he worked he felt a scratch at his calf,
a scarlet wound, a whoop of blood. He was hungry;
even his eyes were hungry.
All he saw was red: red snow, red legs of women
in the village rues, red pinwheels of hay.
"It is a wonderful thing
to hurt a human being, something
that lives. It is confoundedly difficult, but after all it is splendid."

Beyond the window, a cave opened
in the trees and led into emptiness,
a yellow you couldn't quite see an end to.
Van Gogh walked into it,
and his body began to shake. It was a color-riot.
He could hear, somewhere, a dog
thumping its tail in the dark.
"How splendid yellow is!" he said.

★

Color was electricity, it turned you blind
if you got hold of it.
It turned you blind if something cold
got hold of you and blistered.
Walls falling toward you.
When you turn color into a weapon,
something gets left over:
a charred body.
What you must do is take the plaster
and turn it to praise
as light turns grass in the evening
into fear gone blind into the hunt.

from Gulf Coast

Method, or Kenneth Koch

◇   ◇   ◇

Sometimes Kenneth Koch's method I guess you'd call it
was to have a general notion of the whole poem
before he started
such as the history of jazz or the boiling point of water
or talking to things that can't talk back
(as he put it) that is apostrophes
whereas my method I guess I'd call it
is to start and go
wherever the poem seems to lead

Sometimes it doesn't lead anywhere
other than to a dead end, and when I turn around
the street has disappeared and I find myself
sitting in a room.
Sometimes it leads somewhere
I have no interest in being
or the way I get there is contrived or silly

I have a face
that stays mostly on the front of my head
while inside my head wheels
are turning with a sound like music heard across water
over which a breeze rises and falls
cooling my face.
I should be nicer to my face
send it on vacation or just let it go relax
over there under that shady maple
Instead I let it carry all kinds of packages
back and forth from my brain to the world

though of course my brain is a part of the world
I should send my brain on vacation too
though it tells me now that I should consider the possibility that it has always been
      on vacation
Tricky brain! in which
the personality skates around
and the moral character rises and sits, rises and sits
and whose doorway at the bottom has a sign
that says . . . there's not enough light to read it.
I wish there were.

Kenneth said Write a poem in which each line begins with
"I wish . . ."
I wish gorilla
I wish squish
I wish *deux-tiers*
I wish onrushing cloudburst
and the hundred thousand one-second-old wishes came pouring forth
and still are pouring forth
like babies in trees and all over the place
in French postcards after World War I
like water streaming down Zeus
like the concept of optimism when it entered human history
like the simile when it said Do not end your poem with me
I am not like The End I am like a doorway
that leads from one thing

to Cincinnati, and who
am I to argue with a simile
I am a man of constant similes
that buzz and jumble as I walk
then shift and ramble as I buzz and jumble
At any moment the similes can line up
to form the log cabin Lincoln
is said to have built with his own similes
I am like a president
I am like a stove
I am President Stove I will chop down
the cherry tree over there on that page
But someone else is already chopping it down

a boy with a mad grin on his face
a glint of impish fire atop his head
Those cherries were too red!
So much for history
History that rolls above us like an onrushing stormcloud
while we below knit booties and adjust our earmuffs

Young Bentley bent over his microscope
and clicked the shutter of his box camera
thus taking the first photographic portrait of a snowflake
which is how he became known as "Snowflake" Bentley
Outside the blizzard came in sideways
like a wall of arrows
That is all you need to know about Snowflake Bentley

Who else would you like to know about?
Whom! Whom! not Who!
There actually was a great Chinese actor named Wang Whom
who immigrated to the United States in the mid-nineteenth century
and found fame and fortune in the theaters of San Francisco
due mainly to his ability to allow his head to detach
from his body and float up and disappear into the dark
The curtain would close to great applause
and when it opened his head was back
but his body was in two halves split right down the middle
Wang Whom never revealed his magic secrets
even to the beautiful young women who lined up toward him
like iron filings toward a magnet
powerful enough to lift President Stove out of his chair
and give him life again as a mountain
struck repeatedly by lightning
That is all you need to know about Wang Whom

Now for some commentary on things that are always horizontal
The earth is always lying down on itself
and whirling
It is totally relaxed and happy to let everything happen to it
as if it were the wisest person who ever lived
the one who never got up from bed

because the bed flew around everywhere anyone would want to go
and had arms and hands and legs and feet
that were those of the wise horizontal bed-person

Lines indicating very fast movement are horizontal
because the horizon is so fast it is just an idea:
Now you see it now you are it
and then 99 percent of every beautiful thing you ever knew
escaped and went back out into the world
where you vaguely remembered it: your mother's smile
in the glint of sunlight on the chrome of a passing car,
her tears in a gust of wind, her apron in the evening air

as if she were a milkmaid standing in Holland
while those silver and gray clouds billow across the sky
over to scarlet and burning violet tinged with gold
just for her and that one moment.

You are next in line, which is exciting,
which is why life is exciting: every moment is another line
you're next in. Or maybe not, for what about when
you don't know what "line" is and "next"? A goat
comes up close and stares at your sleeping face.
The instant you wake up it turns into a statue
that starts out a goat and ends up a banjo,
something you can neither milk nor play.
But it doesn't matter because you started out a man
and ended up a pile of leaves in a different story.
In the library the other piles are saying Shush, they know
it is late autumn, they can tell by the ruddier cheeks
of the girls who come in and, when they see their books are overdue,
stamp their feet in a fit of pique.
They are so cute
that some of the leaf piles shamble across the floor toward their dresses,
but the girls laugh and throw their hair around and dash away.
If only you weren't a pile of leaves, you would run after them and throw yourself on
    them
like a miracle!

That's what it used to be like to be fourteen and surrounded
by miracles that never happened.
At fifteen the miracles started to crackle and at sixteen
they were positively scary—Look, a miracle on the ceiling!
By seventeen a miracle was a car you could ride in
and then one year later drive beyond the limits of consciousness.
The tapioca pudding was there.
You ate it.
The tapioca pudding was gone
but there too.
May I have some more anything?
Why, my fine young man, you can have anything
you want. Here, have this mountain!
Oof, it's too heavy! Do you have a smaller one?
No, only a larger one.
Then no mountain will I have today
and as for the future I cannot say
because I have no idea where I would ever put a mountain.
But, young man, you will become President Stove!
I will? But I don't want to be a president or a stove,
I want to glue a president *to* a stove.
Then go right ahead. Here is the glue.
Now go find a president and a stove.

from *The Sienese Shredder*

The Classical Study (4)

◇ ◇ ◇

I asked the Master in Rochester
how far the music would carry us.

Past the eglantine, the briars and the bloodgrass?
Past the power station in flames, Martyrs' Square,

and Suleiman's Gate? Past the desert snows
and the Arctic sands? Past the missing pages

piled up in dark basements? The mummified hawks?
I asked in the language of sparrows, of

weasels and owls and gem-studded pharaohs
whose gaze is level and calm.

I asked the Master in Rochester
how far the body would carry us.

Past the donut shop and the Lubyanka and beyond?
I asked as we ordered coffee for the journey ahead.

But first a round of billiards,
the Master said, to settle the nerves,

a game where silence matters
above all, or do I mean sound?

from *Fulcrum*

cosmos, late blooming

◇   ◇   ◇

already the warm days taper to a plumate end: sky, where is your featherbed
some portion for me to fall to, in my contused and stricken state
not the extravagant robe I bartered for: tatters, pinked edges, unpressed

lord, I'm a homely child, scrabbling in the midden for my keep
why should you send this strapping gardener, hay in his teeth, to tend me
now that the showy crown begins to dip like a paper saucer

surely he'll not content with corrupted flesh that dismantles daily
so singular this closing act: spectacular ruin, the spark that descends in air
might he find no thrill in this trodden bower.   ragamuffin sum of veins

in my mouth the mausoleum of refusal: everything died inside me
including fish and vegetables, language and lovers, desire, yes, and passion
how could I make room in this crypt for another sorrow: caretaker:

lost man, these brambles part for your boots, denizened to my lot
your hand upon my stem now grasps the last shoots of summer
choose me for your chaplet, sweetheart.   wasted were my early flowers

—*For Haines Eason*

from *Subtropics*

The Rain That Falls Here

◇   ◇   ◇

1

The rain that falls here is lost,
Having meant surely to fall somewhere else,

Somewhere that's already green.
Like always, like last season,

Like next season—someplace rich with green.
Water knows what to do

And wants a comfortable life
Like anyone.

This time, its instructions get mixed up.
The wind, just to do something different

And as a joke, indifferent and bored,
Carries it here. Pelicans get lost

This same way, blown off course from California.
They get caught standing on the highway medians

Not knowing what to do as the cars speed by.
Like rain, pelicans make the news that evening.

2

The green that the rain saw and meant to feed—
That easy job it thought to have,

Driving around in those big Cadillac clouds,
Not asking anyone for directions—looking down,

The green it thought it saw was something else here.
The green it saw was spray paint and mirage,

Old glass, tired plastic, turquoise and roadkill.
As it turns out, the green that lives here is hard,

Dried and full of dirt just as hard. Sometimes
A few green leaves show themselves,

But not easily. A few peach beetles fly around
Carrying green to taunt us,

A few horseflies are green colored. Dried up
Cowponds have some green around the lip

Of their brown shore, and the man-made lakes
Keep some reeds up for decoration.

3

There are golf courses, to be sure, all green,
But nobody is fooled by them.

They don't count in this discussion.
Anything green here is underground, waiting

To come up, a small guerrilla army of grasses
And wildflowers, scrub brush and cactus.

And people. People would turn green and grow
If there were water, plenty of rain.

We're not sure about this, as it has never happened.
But there is something, just under the skin here,

Something more than sweat. There is a green
Inside, waiting to change everything.

People from other places would not know—
They have used up their allotment of green.

But those here, who have waited these centuries,
That layer of skin they can't explain, it's there.

from *The Virginia Quarterly Review*

"then let fall your horrible pleasure"

◇　◇　◇

physicists live alone in the woods they build fires they burn the limbs of their
numbers

they have pink eyes incantations woeful black tea they scratch

cursed figures in the dirt living forms haunt their geometry they join the wind in
tearing

their rags and mortal hair they forage

on the moist floor of the sky the river holds silt and stars they cup their palms

and drink its long equation they slaughter eternity for its soft meat and its fur

they are very hungry like God who is made of dark matter and wears a thorny
nebula and is everything

that has lost the formula for stopping itself

the tree of the mind its infrastructure bathed in artificial light

a decaying city giant televisions traffic all possible

futures God the infinite subway God the player of many fiddles

and physicists are such poor dancers their limbs go everywhere at once who
hasn't

N A P

lost the formula devoid of rhythm

ιeir awkward striving they are made

en naked which is not often

wering this convinces Presbyterians of

when they see one in the scrub pines

'in the summer beyond

ςht you can listen from your porch

/ at the monolith

from *Gulf Coast*

Three Lanterns

◇   ◇   ◇

There's our son at the end of my hook
    riding over the Detroit River

where Tecumseh's still rowing
    towards his oblivion.

This boy we're casting to the land
    of the leaping frogs.

My lass lives on the floor
    where the fish are frying,

her spine snapped in half
    the way a Milky Way might.

She squares her thumbs and fingers together,
    frames for our son

a picture window to climb through

    ★

Eighteen months with us,
    and our dark-skinned son

still has pockets sewn over his clothes.
    They're filled with stones

that keep a boy underwater,
      his vowels bubbling up to us.

With our brooms and hockey sticks,
      we're swatting away

city streetlights that followed him here,
      those bulbs that bow

and peck at his back.

                    ★

My love's trying to stop the chiming,
      her fingers so singular

since that one dark bell
      is ringing again in her neck.

I hollow this house while she sleeps,
      take my time and chisel

the proper curve so our canoe
      cuts easy through rough water.

My lass is a sweet tomahawk
      for the scalping

of moons and runaway boys.

                    ★

We press four hands over our son's
      mouth when he sleeps

so his body blows up and floats.
      We nail our stakes in the yard

to keep him
      tethered to this world.

See how he splashes
      in summer when he knocks

his mouth against moon water.
      See how we paint with one finger

bright horses across his ribs,
      and rivers on the outside

streaming down his arms.

      ★

Sometimes we sketch with smoke
      a door just over

that rock in our boy's chest. You can hear it
      rusty when he knocks

on our bedroom door. We take the scent
      that falls from him—

baby powder, gun powder—into our skulls
      because we live in an empty house,

and in each bedroom there's a bell
      ringing under the covers

where a child might live.

      ★

We sledge the stake in our yard,
      then let the line out slowly

until our son's way up there
      where the moon makes

a lovely mess of him.
      When my wife and I

are overwhelmed with this,
>we beat our skulls upon the moon,

and it empties over the earth.
>I tell you, when we kiss,

even the little bell in my love's neck
>jingles, it rhythms,

it makes a lovely sound.

from *Ploughshares*

American

◊   ◊   ◊

First time and only time I met LeRoi
we were standing at the Five Spot bar—summer '61:
he was drunk, disgracefully so, which is why

he deigned to talk to me in my white oxford shirt
and hair fluffed up for a future
ivy-league career: I hadn't yet read *The Toilet*

or *The Slave*, I'd only been fucked twice
by two girls from Queens who thought
they were already over the hill. I hadn't yet

thrown a brick through IBM's window,
been gassed at Rockefeller Center—maybe once
I'd climbed the stairs to the War Resisters League,

picked up an A. J. Muste pamphlet or two.
I might have lived on meringue pies
at the Automat, worked the register at Gristede's.

I remember most of what happened, since
I was sixteen, self-assured, sensitive in the worst way—
no one had even laid a hand on me

yet—but then he raised his black turtleneck
to show me the swollen welts on his ribs
where a cop had throttled him, and I had the gall

to insist, "I'm not like that: I'm no racist."
"You just want me to like you," he shrugged,
then the second set began. The next man I met

that tanked up on rage was Archie Shepp.
Every riot you could think of had burned
a putrid city down. For my thirtieth birthday,

he played two short cuts, breathy mid-range
off-pitch squawks, shouted the drummer off stage,
then gave us that stare since there was no one

else to look at, to look at what we'd become.

from *Brilliant Corners*

The Aurora
of the New Mind

◇　◇　◇

There had been rain throughout the province
Cypress & umbrella pines in a palsy of swirling mists
Bent against the onshore whipping winds

I had been so looking forward to your silence
What a pity it never arrived

The uniforms of arrogance had been delivered only
That morning to the new ambassador & his stable of
lovers
The epaulettes alone would have made a lesser man weep

But I know my place & I know my business
& I know my own mind so it never occurred to me

To listen as you recited that litany of automatic
miseries
Familiar to all victims of class warfare & loveless
circumstance
By which I mean of course you & your kind

But I know my place & I know my business & baby
I know my own grieving summer mind

Still I look a lot like Scott Fitzgerald tonight with
my tall

Tumbler of meander & bourbon & mint just clacking my
ice
To the noise of the streetcar ratcheting up some
surprise

I had been so looking forward to your silence
& what a pity it never arrived

Now those alpha waves of desire light up the horizon
Just the way my thoughts all blew wild-empty as you
stood
In the doorway to leave   *in the doorway to leave*

Yet I know my place & I know my business & I know those
Melodies *melodies* & the music of my own mind

from *The Southern Review*

World News

◊   ◊   ◊

[an account of Baudelaire's "Le Voyage"]

1.

Firelight on water.
Equatorial calms.
A cumulus cloud
that loses itself
in the Atlantic deeps.

For a boy in love with war games, globes
and aerial maps, the world is as wide
as an appetite, and wider still
when late at night it's lit by a stylus
penlight beam.
                          So who's to blame
if on such nights we're carried away,
our tempers blooded by the tidal washings
of a satellite feed, our dreams afloat
on a moonless finger's length of sea?

Some are drawn to escape the ethers
of suburban life; others the Freudian
cradle's grave; still others, stargazers
stoned on a woman's astrological eyes,
are cuffed to the mainmast of her bed.

But the traveler is a different breed.

Leaning against the wet zinc of a seaside bar,
he answers each time someone asks:

"So where you off to now?"
"Home."
"Where's home?"
"Wherever it is, whenever I get there, no one takes me in."

Like some new conscript
cleaning the breach
of an M-16,
he imagines himself
(in body armor)
advancing atop an M1A1
Abrams through
Al-Oa'im, Anah, Haditha, Hit.

2.

Killing time, we imitate
the cast-out top's
gyrations; even in sleep,
the mind is driven
round and round
like a roiling sun
some lunatic angel
                    spins
                        in space.

And soul?

"It's little more
than a fashion model
who finds god limned
in the klieg lights
at a photo op."

3.

Foster feeling, your poppied gaze
is all the lunar tide it takes
to float the deadweight of our days.

So why not empty
your haversack
and from
its hand-stitched
lining draw
a spoonful
of that stardust
you have
smuggled in.

Let mind's eye see what eyes have seen.

4.

"I've seen creosoted Hebron skies,
Afghan peaks that burn all night
like something wired, a Kurdish sun
that radiates the fallout in a no-fly zone.
Yet despite the occasional suicide bomb,
I'm often as bored as folks back home.
Like a wildlife eco-tourist as the tour
winds down, I can't help feel
the last resort was just another rock-heap
bleached by guano and mollusk shells."

5.

Yes, but still,
still . . .

6.

Nothing sparks our daydreams more
than the snapshots we've seen through your eyes:
the hand-carved sybaritic doll, the ninth-century
baldachin throne forged from plundered gold
and bronze, garments it took two years to stitch
in sweatshops in San Salvador, and the walled-in
emperor's palace rooms where cobras charm
their handlers, and women who would save themselves
stain their teeth with pomegranate seed.

"And this you call 'EXPERIENCE?'"

7.

Tell us then,
should we stay or should we go?

"How would I know?
One of you says to wait it out.
Another crouches in the hall and prays
the next Jihad will be the last.
Another is like the Wandering Jew
whose shadow seeks asylum
in the walled-off embassies
of Somewhere Else.

But I'll tell you what the wisest do.
Those lovers of absolute zero
at the bone, they pursue their fate
        through the high-
            rise of a glass
                syringe.

The heart enlightened
like a fire balloon
can find its way
across a Sea of Shades."

8.

SO LET YOUR FREED MIND HOLIDAY IN
THE OLD WORLD CHARM OF MAZATLAN

"And once you've had enough of it
the old-world looks like new,
backtrack through the hellish heat
to cool down in your cruise ship's
air-conditioned rooms."

And after that?

"Whatever's listed on the manifest."

Atacama
Kyzyl-kum
Namib
Gobi
Kalahari
Thar

from *Raritan*

Evening Man

◊   ◊   ◊

The man in bed with me this morning is myself, is me,
The sort of same-sex marriage New York State allows.
Both men believe in infidelity.
Both wish they could annul their marriage vows.

This afternoon I will become the Evening Man,
Who does the things most people only dream about.
He swims around his women like a swan, and spreads his fan.
You can't drink that much port and not have gout.

In point of fact, it is arthritis.
His drinking elbow aches, and he admits to this.
To be a candidate for higher office,
You have to practice drastic openness.

You have to practice looking like thin air
When you become the way you do not want to be,
An ancient head of ungrayed dark brown hair
That looks like dyed fur on a wrinkled monkey.

Of course, the real vacation we will take is where we're always headed.
Presidents have Air Force One to fly them there.
I run for office just to get my dark brown hair beheaded.
I wake up on a slab, beheaded, in a White House somewhere.

Evening Man sits signing bills in the Oval Office headless—
Every poem I write starts or ends like this.

His hands have been chopped off. He signs bills with the mess.
The country is in good hands. It ends like this.

from *The New York Review of Books*

Listen

◇　◇　◇

Everything about you,
my life, is both
make-believe and real.
We are like a couple
working the night shift
in a bomb factory.

Come quietly, one says
to the other
as he takes her by the hand
and leads her
to a rooftop
overlooking the city.

At this hour, if one listens
long and hard,
one can hear a fire engine
in the distance,
but not the cries for help,

just the silence
growing deeper
at the sight of a small child
leaping out of a window
with its nightclothes on fire.

from *The New Yorker*

Tara

◇   ◇   ◇

She stood by the door
of her Virginia farm
pulling a sweater on
the branches
of the dogwood
were bowed
blossoms
loosened
in sudden snow
the deer stood
in mute wonder
at the garden's edge
she slipped the phone
in her pocket
her daughter
unharmed
among
petals gone
she snapped
a branch
a tempest stalled
she felt the boy
she felt the dead
she felt the families
she felt the wind
the deer don't do that

she said
the deer don't do that

from *The New Yorker*

R . T . S M I T H

Pentecost

◇　◇　◇

for John Foster West

Squint-eyed and cunning, its tongue split
like a wishbone, the canebrake sulls up,
cursive spine and the diamonds in spiral
like genetic code,

and Joby frets the Stratocaster, its plastic
the color of a salted ham. A tambourine's
discs shiver, and Brother Pascal wields the Book's
hot gospel like a blunt instrument. This is

spirit. This is bliss. The words from Heaven
would almost strangle you. The Holy Ghost
is a rough customer alright,
and if someone comes for healing touch,

for translation into a mended soul,
a whole body, let him lie beside the altar
all shorn and shocked and willing, sing *amen*, say
grace abounding,

and the current sizzles, the tail beads buzz,
as the road to Zion is not all gleam-gold.
Wind scratching poplar limbs
against cracked board-and-batten says

stormy heart. You can translate any syllable
into yearning, the Lord's will,

as the rattler agitates, this being winter,
his deep sleep stolen by a prophet's

hands clapping, raw notes of "power
in the blood." He's a mean
messenger, unguessable, and Brother Harvey
Robbins now cradling him

has the look of a man ready for crisis.
Come rapture, come venom,
that double ivory stab so quick you're
not sure at first, then certain. It leaves limbs

withered but quickened. For some of us
in the lantern light, in the Carver's Cove
church house where the floor rattles
like a loom room, a coal scuttle:

we know something is coming.
Snake-shakers, Holy Rollers, Faith
Healers from over in Silva or up in Teague,
we feel the wild muscle contract.

It's no cakewalk to dance the devil
down. Uproot and undercut,
but something is coming right
now, something good. Leave your

coppers and dollars in the collection plate.
The moon out there is empty, visible
as a skillet in night sky.
The whoosh of angel feathers is coming,

the serpent's hiss, the new dialect
we will sing to spring sowing, hallelujah.
On a good night the serpent will crown
some beloved brow like braided brocade

and idle there, benign, as we begin
the mortal bargain, breathe the honey air

117

of limber love and behold
as the jaws open for a half-sought kiss.

Crystals in the hourglass glisten and summon,
the weave of bequeathed bliss,
birthright of the cursed helix.
Sister, keep your eye on the cross,

take my hand. The words will come.

from *Notre Dame Review*

Hexagon: On Truth

◇   ◇   ◇

"But must we always, then," the poet will wonder, *"rejoice in regions that are loftier than the truth?"*
—*The Life of the Bee,* by Maurice Maeterlinck
(trans. Alfred Sutro)

Now, in the lab on Mt. Graham, a robot is polishing a mirror. The robot will continue polishing all night. Tomorrow morning it will still be polishing, into the afternoon and into the fall. Then it will be repaired and go back to polishing a winter night. As spring polishes morning. As breath polishes silence.

•

Everything is moving away from everything. Everything shifts red, we shift red, as we draw away from each other. In time we realize we have already left. This is rarefaction. Its inverse: compression. These forces create waves.

•

The backside of this mirror is a honeycomb. Honeycombs are known for their strength in lightness. *I shall confine myself generally to relating what is patent to any one who may gather a swarm into a glass hive.* Bees are known for their devotion to a single task, such as collecting pollen from a field. The front side of the mirror is a hive with a single worker. As long as it polishes, the robot presses itself against itself.

•

The robot polishes the largest mirror ever manufactured. It will be part of a telescope for gathering light from the vineyard of stars. The shape of this mirror is the shape of wine in a spinning glass. For three months it cooled until we could safely put our lips to its lip. We left a wine stain: a galaxy blacked out. Better to put our lips to our lips; better to compress.

•

This is patent: hives are built from the top down, *for we have here an inverted city, hanging down from the sky.* A dense swarm will suspend on a branch or the corner of a hayloft. Slowly this swarm polishes its wax down in the shape of a suspended wineglass. *The bees, however, are not infallible, nor does their certainty appear mechanical. They will commit grave errors at times; they will often leave too much space.*

•

Of the visible forms of light, red is the coolest. Cooling draws us nearer to evenness. Everything cools. Cool air is denser and carries less water, which affords clearer views of the sky. When air becomes too cool, droplets condense on bees' wings, renders them useless. Sunlight reflected through them evaporates them.

•

The robot does a good job. If this mirror were as large as North America, nothing would extend higher than four inches. Cinemas, cornfields, salmon hatcheries, windmills, Mt. Graham, the beehive, all shorter than four inches. As the robot polishes, the mirror draws nearer to uniformity. We are drawing nearer. Good robot.

•

Scientists look for solutions, explorers look everywhere for elsewheres, gather clover from the field. Even such a mirror will find it hard to gain a clear view—*A passing bird, a few drops of rain, a mistake, a cold wind—any one of these may give rise to irremediable disaster.* Bees dance, a robot polishes. Collection, compression. Atmosphere trembles.

•

If a bee returns from the meadow to find her hive moved away, she will hover in the space where the hive should be. She continues until she can't. Until she's exhausted from polishing the air with her wings. Imperfections are inevitable. When the robot stops polishing there will still be imperfections, imperfections smaller than the waves of light. When the image of the robot is indistinguishable from the robot, the robot stops polishing.

•

The bee is above all, a creature of the crowd. When she leaves the hive, she departs from her proper element. She will dive for an instant into flower-filled space, as the swimmer will dive into the sea that is filled with pearls. It behooves her at regular intervals to return and breathe the crowd as the swimmer must return and breathe the air. Isolate her, and she will expire in a few days not of hunger or cold, but of loneliness. If North America were the size of the mirror, the color red would bounce every two feet.

•

As stars die they rarify, redden. These are red giants. Our sun will become a red giant and as it expands it will swallow the earth. We have calculated it would be so large as to hold four million earths. In these calculations, hexagonal chambers of light enclose these many earths. By then no earths will exist, much less many.

•

By fall, the inside of the honeycomb is so filled with honey that the walls reflect light. It is thought that this increase of light calms the bees' compulsion to gather pollen. *They never can look too high. Truth rises as they draw nearer; they draw nearer when they admire . . .* We aren't sure. There is no way to measure calm in bees. And it might be the light of an early sunset, an October evening, the first snowflake blown inside the hive.

•

On the perfect white salt flats at Uyuni, on the day it rains, there is a larger mirror on earth. If the mirror were the size of the salt flats, nothing would extend higher than the height of a bee. Thinness of water over

121

pure white salt makes a hole in the world. Hovering at the right distance above the salt flats, we cannot see the earth—only the space behind, as if our world moved away. We will look down at the space behind, the entire inverse, becoming a dim, even, red. We will keep hovering; we will redden as we draw away.

from *Quarterly West*

Cricket

◇   ◇   ◇

Apocalyptic knucklebone,
   black-letter font
so antique among the modern things,

you cause the room to flinch
   at my intrusion,
quaver in corners, trill

in mortised triplets the crowded
   heavy boots,
sodden mat, stiff thicket of broom.

Your ceremonial frequencies
   abrade what I might choose
to forget, lonely scrape of a chair

under fluorescent morgue-light
   of winter kitchen,
wince as the soul divides.

Hasp of flesh, sear fact
   through which your trespass,
your vesper curfew gnaws.

from *Meridian*

The Shoe

◇   ◇   ◇

Each time I relived it, after the worst
was over, I'd say to myself, as if my fate
would solace me,
"at least I'll never have to do this again."
It is true that I'll never have to kiss his
dying hands, now dead. I'll never have
to find where he left his coffeemug, now mine.

I'll never have to wash his hair or repair
his typewriter or stock the medicine stand.
I'll never even have to find places
that can use his clothes because
some friend—I don't remember who—
did that for me when I could not. I
distributed his portrait, I picked up his poems.

I thanked friends and children for helping me
hold on. I made braids out of dead funeral
flowers to border the rooms where
once he breathed and took on the heavy
chores, gladly, of loving me. I sprinkled
one teaspoon of his ashes on our bereft bed
and slept with them. They scourged my body.

But when that single shoe, the mate I thought
had got sent off with its partner, showed up
today, alone, crouching behind the couch, alive
with Effie's oppulent Turkish angora fur, I knew

solace was something I could neither seek nor find. Oh beloved! I know I am an old woman. But I cannot live in your shoe.

from *Harvard Review*

Divide and Conquer

◊   ◊   ◊

The cells divide. The cells that will not die
divide too well and so they multiply.
They kill the host to keep themselves alive.

The blood goes bad. In vain physicians try
to purge the veins with drugs the cells defy.
The cells divide. The cells that will not die

mutate anew. The hardy few survive.
The few recruit the many teeming by.
They kill the host to keep themselves alive.

They colonize the nodes from neck to thigh.
The tumors grow, and scanners never lie.
The cells divide. The cells that will not die

stifle the very organs where they thrive.
Blind, stupid things—their purpose gone awry—
they kill the host to keep themselves alive.

Exploding through the flesh, they multiply,
but immortality eludes them. Why?
The cells divide, the cells that will not die
kill the host to keep themselves alive.

from *The Hudson Review*

CHAD SWEENEY

The Sentence

◇   ◇   ◇

The bones of Marcel Duchamp
laid end to end
reach all the way

to the bottom of this hill
where a little slab of concrete
bridges one

obscurity to another
and Mr. Duchamp seems pleased
the way I've placed his jaw

in relation to the atlas
his wisdom teeth
commanding long sharp shadows

though it's noon
(the midnight of day)
and we've nowhere to go

and the oblique syntax of bones
repeats its inquiry
in the language of the world

from *New American Writing*

The Troubadours etc.

◇　◇　◇

Just for this evening, let's not mock them.
Not their curtsies or cross-garters
Or ever recurring pepper trees in their gardens
Promising, promising.

At least they had ideas about love.

All day we've driven past cornfields, past cows poking their heads
Through metal contraptions to eat.
We've followed West 84, and what else?
Irrigation sprinklers fly past us, huge wooden spools in the fields,
Lounging sheep, telephone wires,
Yellowing flowering shrubs.

Before us, above us, the clouds swell, layers of them,
The violet underneath of clouds.
Every idea I have is nostalgia. Look up:
There is the sky that passenger pigeons darkened and filled—
Darkened for days, eclipsing sun, eclipsing all other sound with the thunder of
　　　their wings.
After a while, it must have seemed that they followed
Not instinct or pattern but only
One another.

When they stopped, Audubon observed,
They broke the limbs of stout trees by the sheer weight of their numbers.

And when we stop we'll follow—what?
Our *hearts?*

The Puritans thought that we are granted the ability to love
Only through miracle,
But the troubadours knew how to burn themselves through,
How to make themselves shrines to their own longing.
The spectacular was never behind them.

Think of days of those scarlet-breasted, blue-winged birds above you.
Think of me in the garden, humming
Quietly to myself in my blue dress,
A blue darker than the sky above us, a blue dark enough for storms,
Though cloudless.

At what point is something gone completely?
The last of the sunlight is disappearing
Even as it swells and waves.

Just for this evening, won't you put me before you
Until I'm far enough away you can
Believe in me?

Then try, try to come closer—
My wonderful and less than.

from *Meridian*

National Security

◇   ◇   ◇

I said, "I want to go home." "I told you, we have no home,"
Anne said. "What happened to our home?" I said. "The government
took it," she said. "What for?" I said. "They said it was for
strategic reasons," she said. And, thus, we commenced our roaming.
Mostly we stayed at campsites along the way. We had a tent and
sleeping bags, a couple of pots and pans. I was confused about what
had happened to us, but I also liked the adventure. Once a man
came over and said that he and his wife would like to share their
dinner with us. Anne said her husband wasn't feeling well. I said,
"I feel great." We sat around their campfire and talked. The man
said he used to be a dentist, but now he was a goldminer. "You
should've been taking those little gold caps out of people's
mouths all along. You'd be rich now," I said. Anne ploughed
her elbow into my ribs. "We're headed for the Klondike," his
wife said. "It's best to stay out of the strategic zones," Anne
said. They nodded in unison. "But I still don't know where they
are," I said. They all looked at me, but didn't say anything.
We ate some awful, strange meat and some baked beans, at least I
think that's what they were. Later that night I was sick. In the
morning when we had been on the road about three hours a band of
Indians came riding toward us. "What are we supposed to do?" I
said to Anne. "They've risen up all over the country. They're
on the warpath. They're going to take over the government," she
said. "But what about us right now?" I said. "Just be nice,"
she said. When they came alongside of the car, Anne stopped
and rolled down her window. "Howdy, fellow Americans," she said.
"Can you tell us how to get to Topeka?" he said. "Sure, that's
easy," she said and proceeded to give him directions. "That's
most helpful," he said. "Have a good day." We drove on into

the glaring sun. "Where are we going?" I said. "Do I look like I know where we're going? I just want to get away as far as we can," she said. "What about our old friends?" I said. "You'll just have to make new ones," she said. "Patagonia, is that where we're going?" I said. "No, we're not going to Patagonia. I don't know where we're going," she said. "We're getting low on gas and I don't think there's going to be a station for a long time," I said. "Then we'll have to walk," she said. I was beginning to see how crazed she was and it frightened me. "We don't have anything to eat," I said. "You can kill a jackrabbit," she said. There was an old shepherd up ahead moving his flock across the road. When we pulled to a stop, she said, "Get out and grab one of those sheep and throw it in the backseat." I said, "I'm not going to do that. There's no way." She looked at me, then opened her door, and went and grabbed a sheep around its waist and tried to heft it up. She dropped it and tried again. It took all her strength to drag it over to the car. She finally managed to stuff it in the backseat before the shepherd saw what she had done. He pounded on her window and hit it with his staff. "A curse on you. I put a curse on you!" he shouted. She rolled down her window and yelled back at him, "National Security. It's for your own good."

from *VOLT*

On Captivity

◇　◇　◇

Being all Stripped as Naked as We were Born, and endeavor-
ing to hide our Nakedness, these Cannaballs took [our] Books,
and tearing out the Leaves would give each of us a Leaf to cover
us . . .

—Jonathan Dickinson, 1699

At the hands now
　　　of their captors, those
　　　　　they've named *savages,*
　　　do they say the word itself
savagely—hissing

that first letter,
　　　the serpent's image,
　　　　　releasing
　　　thought into speech?
For them now,

everything is flesh
　　　as if their thoughts, made
　　　　　suddenly corporeal,
　　　reveal even more
their nakedness—

the shame of it:
　　　their bodies rendered
　　　　　plain as the natives'—
　　　homely and pale,
their ordinary sex,

the secret illicit hairs
        that do not (cannot)
            cover enough.
        This is how they are brought,
naked as newborns,

to knowledge. Adam and Eve
        in the New World,
                they have only the Bible
        to cover them. Think of it:
a woman holding before her

the torn leaves of *Genesis,*
        and a man covering himself
                with the Good Book's
        frontispiece—his own name
inscribed on the page.

            from *Five Points*

Thomas Hardy

◇ ◇ ◇

There's not a chance.
Too late, he says. But it's never too late
for the poetry of regret.

Pines thicken with this rain.
Always, under complaint,
storm clouds ride above

an ancient forest.
A child close to the earth
listens to the slow revolving of

accidents. Already the child knows
he is a ghost
and must practice becoming himself—

the cliff rising above him will not stop.
He's not one ghost but many,
and there's not enough pity in the world for them.

from *Barrow Street*

DARA WIER

Faithful

◇   ◇   ◇

You come as close as the skin on my face,
As if you were a sure enough wind for me to walk into.
In woodgrain on a doorframe of a door I walk out of
You wander and I wander with you.
With luciferin, luciferase and oxygen you light the way.
A mid-summer's late evening scatters you so
That by midnight all of the stars that surround us
By morning by cresting by curving by blazing,
You are light that has passed through my eyes.
I see you in profile as if sharpened and stenciled
Examining creases in the palm of my hand.
Exchanging places in ground fog with black flares.
What is this translucence you've dropped between us,
When will a sure enough wind arrive to blow this curtain aside?

from *The American Poetry Review*

Light

◇　◇　◇

Another drought morning after a too brief dawn downpour,
uncountable silvery glitterings on the leaves of the withering maples—

I think of a troop of the blissful blessed approaching Dante,
"a hundred spheres shining," he rhapsodizes, "the purest pearls . . ."

then of the frightening, brilliant, myriad gleam in my lamp
of the eyes of the vast swarm of bats I found once in a cave,

a chamber whose walls seethed with a spaceless carpet of creatures,
their cacophonous, keen, insistent, incessant squeakings and squealings

churning the warm, rank, cloying air; of how one,
perfectly still among all the fitfully twitching others,

was looking straight at me, gazing solemnly, thoughtfully up
from beneath the intricate furl of its leathery wings

as though it couldn't believe I was there, or was trying to place me,
to situate me in the gnarl we'd evolved from, and now,

the trees still heartrendingly asparkle, Dante again,
this time the way he'll refer to a figure he meets as "the life of . . ."

not the soul, or person, the *life*, and once more the bat, and I,
our lives in that moment together, our lives, our *lives*,

his with no vision of celestial splendor, no poem,
mine with no flight, no unblundering dash through the dark,

his without realizing it would, so soon, no longer exist,
mine having to know for us both that everything ends,

world, after-world, even their memory, steamed away
like the film of uncertain vapor of the last of the luscious rain.

from *The New Yorker*

Passing Scenes
(While Reading Basho)

◇　◇　◇

I am traveling by train
to the city,
                    I am traveling
in brilliant sleep
into the past

Meantime composing
a letter
to my inner no one

    There were hives at the
edge of a wood

The mind shines
    in the
    window

The most beautiful house I ever died in

Everything's imaginary

When I hear the dawn gulls cry
even in New York
I long for New York—

from *Field*

[Language exists because]

◇   ◇   ◇

Language exists because nothing exists between those
who express themselves. All language is therefore
a language of prayer. Held in the dark, without sleep. Faith

is the confession that there exists that
wherein one is faithless. Wherein faith isolates a position of value there
       exists
two essential hells. The one you are in.

And the one you are after.
Sound is positioned in the other and is poetic because it is unspoken.
    Incidence
after *incidere* is positioned *in* from *cadere, to fall.* The point is incident

when it falls on the line is incident when it *passes through* a point even in
the dark
is only an idealized limit of a smaller and smaller presence. The heart
which is an orgasm. A long dagger. The prayer exists

because it is positioned. In that presence
wherein the heart is expressed. Wherein sound is incident to the heart
exists. I am not asking you to die for me. Say you will die for me.

from *Phoebe*

Sepsis

◇ ◇ ◇

The fog has yet to lift, God, and still the bustle
of buses and garbage trucks. God, I have coveted
sleep. I have wished to find an empty bed

in the hospital while on call. I have placed
my bodily needs first, left nurses to do
what I should have done. And so, the antibiotics

sat on the counter. They sat on the counter
under incandescent lights. No needle was placed
in the woman's arm. No IV was started. It sat there

on the counter waiting. I have coveted sleep, God,
and the toxins I studied in Bacteriology took hold
of Your servant. When the blood flowered

beneath her skin, I shocked her, placed the paddles
on her chest, her dying body convulsing each time.
The antibiotics sat on the counter, and shame

colored my face, the blood pooling in my cheeks
like heat. And outside, the stars continued falling
into place. And the owl kept talking without listening.

And the wind kept sweeping the streets clean.
And the heart in my chest stayed silent.
How could I have known that I would never forget,

that early some mornings, in the waking time,
the fog still filling the avenues, that the image
of her body clothed in sweat would find me?

I have disobeyed my Oath. I have caused harm.
I have failed the preacher from the Baptist Church.
Dear God, how does a sinner outlast the sin?

from *The Virginia Quarterly Review*

The Dead from Iraq

◇　◇　◇

They come back and stand in our midst,
young men in camouflage, heads shaved,
with undecided smiles, puzzled eyes.
We seldom happen to perceive them—

partly because we never really wish to;
vague sentinels, stiff at attention,
there in the corners of our vision
among the reeds or trees or graves.

This morning, as the season shifts again,
I'm more morose, half-conscious of their presence,
their numbers and their distribution,

real and not real, somber and too silent,
like phantom limbs that, after amputation,
we slowly talk ourselves out of using.

from *ABZ: A Poetry Magazine*

No Forgiveness Ode

◇　◇　◇

The husband wants to be taken back
into the family after behaving terribly,
but nothing can be taken back,
not the leaves by the trees, the rain
by the clouds. You want to take back
the ugly thing you said, but some shrapnel
remains in the wound, some mud.
Night after night Tybalt's stabbed
so the lovers are ground in mechanical
aftermath. Think of the gunk that never
comes off the roasting pan, the goofs
of a diamond cutter. But wasn't it
electricity's blunder into inert clay
that started this whole mess, the I-
echo in the head, a marriage begun
with a fender bender, a sneeze,
a mutation, a raid, an irrevocable
fuckup. So in the meantime: epoxy,
the dog barking at who knows what,
signals mixed up like a dumped-out tray
of printer's type. Some piece of you
stays in me and I'll never give it back.
The heart hoards its thorns
just as the rose profligates.
Just because you've had enough
doesn't mean you wanted too much.

from *The Paris Review* and *Poetry Daily*

From "Book of Hours"

◇   ◇   ◇

The light here leaves you
lonely, fading

as does the dusk
that takes too long

to arrive. By morning
the mountain moving

a bit closer to the sun.

This valley belongs
to no one—

except birds who name
themselves by their songs

in the dawn.
What good

are wishes, if they aren't
used up?

The lamp of your arms.

The brightest
blue beneath the clouds—

We guess
at what's next.

unlike the mountain

who knows it
in the bones, a music

too high
to scale.

              ★   ★   ★

The burnt,
blurred world

where does it end—

The wind
kicks up the scent

from the stables
where horseshoes hold

not just luck, but
beyond. But

weight. But a body

that itself burns,
begs to run.

The gondola quits just
past the clouds.

The telephone poles
tall crosses in the road.

Let us go
each, into the valley—

inside out, let the world
itch—for once—

★   ★   ★

Black like an eye

bruised night brightens
by morning, yellow

then gray—
a memory.

What the light was like.

All day the heat a heavy,
colored coat.

I want to lie
down like the lamb—

down & down
till gone—

shorn of its wool.
The cool

of setting & rising
in this valley,

the canyon between us
shoulders our echoes.

Moan, & make way.

★   ★   ★

The sun's small fury
feeds me.

Wind dying down.

We delay, & dither
then are lifted

into it, brightness
all about—

O setting.
O the music

as we soar
is small, yet sating.

What you want—

Nobody, or nothing
fills our short journeying.

Above even the birds,
winging heavenward,

the world is hard
to leave behind

or land against—
must end.

I mean to make it.

Turning slow beneath
our feet,

finding sun, seen
from above,

this world looks
like us—mostly

salt, dark water.

★   ★   ★

It's death there
is no cure for—

life the long
disease.

If we're lucky.

Otherwise, short
trip beyond.

And below.

Noon,
growing shadow.

I chase the quiet
round the house.

Soon the sound—

wind wills
its way against

the panes. Welcome
the rain.

Welcome
the moon's squinting

into space.
The trees

bow like priests.

The storm lifts
up the leaves.

Why not sing.

from *Poetry*

CONTRIBUTORS' NOTES AND COMMENTS

TOM ANDREWS was born in Charleston, West Virginia, in 1961. His poetry collections include *The Hemophiliac's Motorcycle* (University of Iowa Press, 1994), winner of the Iowa Poetry Prize, and *The Brother's Country* (Persea Books, 1990). He edited collections of criticism on two contemporary pocts: *On William Stafford: The Worth of Local Things* (University of Michigan Press) and *The Point Where All Things Meet: Essays on Charles Wright* (Oberlin College Press), both appearing in 1995. His memoir, *Codeine Diary: True Confessions of a Reckless Hemophiliac* (Harvest Books), appeared in 1999. He died of thrombotic thrombocytopinic purpura in London, England, on July 19, 2001. A posthumous volume, *Random Symmetries: The Collected Poems of Tom Andrews,* was published by Oberlin the following year.

RALPH ANGEL was born in Seattle, Washington, in 1951. He has written four books of poetry: *Exceptions and Melancholies: Poems 1986–2006,* winner of the 2007 PEN USA Poetry Award (Sarabande Books, 2006); *Twice Removed* (Sarabande Books, 2001); *Neither World* (Miami University Press, 1995); and *Anxious Latitudes* (Wesleyan University Press, 1986). His translation of Federico García Lorca's *Poema del cante jondo / Poem of the Deep Song* appeared from Sarabande in 2006. He is the Edith R. White Distinguished Professor at the University of Redlands.

Of "Exceptions and Melancholies," Angel writes: "Some weeks after I made the poem, I found the title for it in a letter from George Sand to Gustave Flaubert. Eventually, it became the title of the entire collection, and I used a piece of George Sand's letter as the book's epigraph: 'I fall into melancholies of honey and roses which are none the less melancholy. . . . I assure you that there is only one pleasure: learning what one does not know, and one happiness: loving the exceptions.'"

RAE ARMANTROUT was born in Vallejo, California, in 1947. She has lived in California her whole life. She teaches poetry at the University of California, San Diego. Her most recent collection of poems is *Next Life* (Wesleyan University Press, 2007). Her *Collected Prose* came out from Singing Horse Press in the same year. Wesleyan also published *Up to Speed* (2004) and *Veil: New and Collected Poems* (2001).

Armantrout writes: "'Framing' was composed on a beautiful day in an especially wet year in San Diego (2005). The usually dry hills were 'articulated' by or with flowers, and migrating butterflies swarmed everywhere. I had recently learned of Robert Creeley's death. It seemed like a particularly lousy day on which to be dead."

JOHN ASHBERY was born in Rochester, New York, in 1927. His most recent books are *Where Shall I Wander* (Ecco Press, 2005), *A Worldly Country* (Ecco, 2007), and *Notes from the Air: Selected Later Poems* (Ecco, 2007). His translation of Pierre Reverdy's *Haunted House* was published by Black Square Editions and *The Brooklyn Rail* in 2007. He has also translated the selected poems of Pierre Martory: *The Landscapist* (Sheep Meadow Press, 2008). Volume one of his *Collected Poems* (Library of America) will appear in fall 2008. Since 1990 he has been the Charles P. Stevenson, Jr., Professor of Languages and Literature at Bard College. He edited the inaugural volume in the *Best American Poetry* series in 1988.

Ashbery writes: "'Pavane pour Helen Twelvetrees' alludes to Ravel's lovely 'Pavane pour une infante défunte' (Pavane for a dead infanta). Helen Twelvetrees had a brief career as a leading actress in early talkies, often as a tough but vulnerable blonde. I was remembering her in a 1930 movie, *Her Man,* directed by Tay Garnett, in which she played opposite Phillips Holmes. It took place in Havana. Holmes was a sailor and Twelvetrees a dancehall hostess. I saw it at the Cinémathèque in Paris in the late fifties; David Thomson in an essay on Tay Garnett mentions it as a 'lost movie.' It could well have been lost since I saw it due to the Cinémathèque's rather careless housekeeping habits. I remember the line about Saint Patrick's Day from the film. Of course, none of this 'explains' the poem; the poem will have to do that."

JOSHUA BECKMAN was born in New Haven, Connecticut, in 1971. His six books of poetry include *Things Are Happening* (*The American Poetry Review* / Honickman First Book Prize, 1998), *Shake* (Wave Books, 2006), and most recently a self-published collaboration with Anthony McCann and Matthew Rohrer, *Gentle Reader!* He divides his time between Brooklyn, New York, and Seattle, Washington.

Of his untitled poem, Beckman writes: "This poem is part of a larger series called *Let the People Die.* The series, which approximates a sonnet cycle, was written while I was living in Staten Island, New York, and this poem (like many of the others) was written on the Staten Island Ferry."

MARVIN BELL was born in New York City in 1937. His nineteenth book, *Mars Being Red,* appeared from Copper Canyon Press in 2007. Previous collections of poetry include seven books from Atheneum and five from Copper Canyon, including *The Book of the Dead Man* (1994), *Nightworks* (2000), and *Rampant* (2004). Retired from the Iowa Writers' Workshop, he serves on the faculty of the brief-residency MFA program based in Oregon at Pacific University, and performs with the bassist Glen Moore of the jazz group Oregon. He and his wife live in Iowa City, Iowa, and Port Townsend, Washington.

Bell writes: "'Poseur' started out in 1992 as a much longer poem beginning with the line, 'I recently committed suicide but didn't die.' That was two years after the first of my 'dead man poems' appeared in a book—and two years before *The Book of the Dead Man.* In this poem, too, I felt at home in the overarching sensibility of a man alive and dead at the same time. While putting together the collection, *Mars Being Red,* I realized that 'Poseur' is still of the moment. I remain partial to the imagination that has a philosophical tilt to it "

CHARLES BERNSTEIN was born in Manhattan in 1950. He has published more than twenty collections of poetry and three collections of essays, including *Girly Man, My Way: Speeches and Poems* and *With Strings,* from the University of Chicago Press; *Republics of Reality: Poems 1975–1995,* from Sun & Moon Press; and *Shadowtime* (Green Integer). From 1978 to 1981 he coedited, with Bruce Andrews, *L=A=N=G=U=A=G=E* magazine. In the 1990s, he cofounded and directed the Poetics Program at the State University of New York, Buffalo. Bernstein is the codirector, with Al Filries, of PennSound (writing.upenn.edu/pennsound) and editor of the Electronic Poetry Center (epc.buffalo.edu). He is Donald T. Regan Professor of English at the University of Pennsylvania.

Bernstein writes: "'Hay(na)ku' is a form invented by Eileen Tabios in 2003. Structure is one, then two, then three words per line. For instance, Tom Beckett's 'Language / is the / fabric of consciousness.' Louis Zukofsky often counted by words rather than by syllables. Think of his many poems with five words per line. You can feel the deliberate rhythm of word by word. Then of course there are William Carlos Williams and Robert Creeley. Not fixed counts in their work but words / weight / rhythm. *I count I guess but I guess I count differently.* That's why I wrote this note in ten-word sentences.

"Fixed forms do not have to be traditional or 'received.' And if OuLiPo is mostly hard, counting to three is not. Compare haiku form of 5, 7, and 5 syllable lines. Three lines, well not always, but the last gotta swerve. Or so Koji Kawamoto explains in *Poetics of Japanese Verse.* I met him at the Porter Institute, Israel, in 1997. We were at the 'Poetics of Avant-Garde Poetry' conference. I wrote a poem for him that sort of connects. Syllable counting's—'Tel Aviv so far / Koji waxes avant-garde. / Haiku's news stays new'—supple, but whole words also measure."

CIARAN BERRY was born in Dublin, Ireland, in 1971. He has lived in the United States for the last eleven years and currently teaches in New York University's expository writing program. His first full-length volume, *The Sphere of Birds,* won the 2007 Crab Orchard competition and was published in March 2008 by Southern Illinois University Press. The same volume was published in Ireland and the United Kingdom by the Gallery Press.

Of "Electrocuting an Elephant," Berry writes: "This poem evolved out of a fragment of a larger discarded work centering on the history of Coney Island. The part about the execution, which had haunted me since I first saw it in Ken Burns's documentary on the island, was the only part of the sequence that seemed viable, and I'd been carrying it around for a while, taking it out occasionally and then putting it away. The crueler aspects of my schooling in rural Ireland have never left me, and eventually the image of the elephant being walked very solemnly, very purposefully, to her death began to attach itself to the image of the boy dragged by the ear who later tries to name the birds. Bartholomew came along after that and, I think, out of something I'd written in a note-book. Slowly the various strands of the poem began to gel. I didn't think of it as a political piece at the time, but whenever I look at it now, I realize that what was going on in the world was there, in some small sense, informing what I'd never thought of as allegorical. The poems know more than we do, I suppose."

FRANK BIDART was born in Bakersfield, California, in 1939. He didn't escape until 1957, when he began to study at the University of California, Riverside. "Escape" is an exaggeration; childhood and youth take too long, perhaps everywhere. He began graduate work at Harvard in 1962, studying with Reuben Brower and Robert Lowell. His books include *Star Dust* (2005) and *Desire* (1997), both from Farrar, Straus and Giroux. He is the coeditor of Robert Lowell's *Collected Poems* (2003) and has taught at Wellesley College since 1972. He lives in Cambridge, Massachusetts.

ROBERT BLY was born in Minnesota in 1926. His first book, *Silence in the Snowy Fields,* was published by Wesleyan University Press in 1962. His second book, *The Light Around the Body* (Harper & Row), won the National Book Award in 1967. Among his other major books are *Sleepers Joining Hands* (1973), *The Man in the Black Coat Turns* (1980), *What Have I Ever Lost by Dying* (1990), *Morning Poems* (1997), *The Night Abraham Called to the Stars* (2001), and *My Sentence Was a Thousand Years of Joy* (2005). His books of prose include *Iron John* (1990), *The Sibling Society* (1996), and *The Maiden King* (with Marion Woodman, 1998). His selected translations, *The Winged Energy of Delight,* appeared from HarperCollins in 2004. A volume of translations of Hafez, *Angels Knocking at the Tavern Door* (with Leonard Lewisohn), will be published by the same publisher in 2008.

Bly writes: "'Wanting Sumptuous Heavens' is written in a form called the *ramage*. This form requires eight lines of roughly ten syllables each. The poem is held together, so to speak, by certain particular sounds that are repeated in the course of the poem. In this case, the sound *um*, as in 'grumbles' and 'summer,' appears in each of the couplets twice and sometimes more, so that even though the poem does not offer any end rhymes, it is built on a number of interior rhymes.

"I like the delicious flavor of the small sounds reappearing like raisins in a muffin."

JOHN CASTEEN was born in Hayward, California, in 1971. He serves on the editorial staff of *The Virginia Quarterly Review* and teaches writing and literature at Sweet Briar College and the University of Virginia. He lives in Earlysville, Virginia, where, for ten years after graduating from the Iowa Writers' Workshop, he was self-employed as a designer and builder of custom furniture. His first book, *Free Union,* will appear in spring 2009 from the University of Georgia Press.

Casteen writes: "'Night Hunting' was a hard poem to write and to revise to my satisfaction. I worked on it off and on for several years, leaving it alone when I felt too close to it and returning to it when I could be more objective. Most people who write poems do so because they feel called to it, or compelled by some impulse larger than they, and I do, too. To be faithful to that impulse, the poem has to bear on issues larger than memory or circumstance.

"So, it's difficult. One wants to come out of the process with a document that doesn't simply remain personal, relevant only to the writer, but is not so full of portent that it seems bombastic or preachy. It's a fine line to walk, finding one's way between two negatives. All I had to work with here was the feeling of doing what we were doing, contending with the simultaneous rightness and wrongness of it. I tried to figure out what a poem could make of that besides autobiography."

LAURA CRONK was born in New Castle, Indiana, in 1977. She has lived in the New York area since 2002, currently with her husband in Jersey City.

Cronk writes: "I'm from the rural Midwest, and driving alone at night there after a snowfall is a peculiar, otherworldly experience. 'Entering' was, at first, a very long poem. I've tried to whittle it down to its essences: snow, death, and mice."

KATE DANIELS was born in Richmond, Virginia, in 1953. Her books of poems are *The White Wave* (University of Pittsburgh Press, 1984, winner of the Starrett Prize), *The Niobe Poems* (Pittsburgh, 1989), and *Four Testimonies* (Louisiana State University Press, 1998, Southern Messenger Series). She has edited the selected poems of Muriel Rukeyser, a volume of essays on Robert Bly, and a forthcoming anthology of poems about psychoanalysis and psychotherapy. She is an associate dean at Vanderbilt University, where she has taught since 1995.

Of "Homage to Calvin Spotswood," Daniels writes: "I was born into the white working class in the South in the middle of the twentieth century—a fact that continues to bear its imprint in my poetry, even in late middle age. A large number of my poems have focused on the ubiquitous racism that dominated that time and place. 'Homage to Calvin Spotswood' is a recent example of one way in which this material presented itself to me imaginatively."

LYDIA DAVIS was born in 1947 in Northampton, Massachusetts, and grew up there and in Austria, New York City, and Vermont. She is the author of one novel, *The End of the Story* (Farrar, Straus and Giroux, 1995), and four collections of stories, including, most recently, *Varieties of Disturbance* (FSG, 2007), a finalist for the National Book Award. Among her many translations is the new version of *Swann's Way,* by Marcel Proust, which was awarded the French-American Translation Prize for 2003. On the faculty of SUNY Albany, and a fellow of the New York State Writers Institute, she is at work translating Flaubert's *Madame Bovary.*

Of "Men," Davis writes: "I have always thought of this piece as a story, although it does, like many of my paragraph-long pieces, sit in a territory somewhere between story and prose poem (or meditation, logical argument, reverie, rant, etc.). It was written during a period in which I had found myself not writing much and had set myself a challenge. I was to write two paragraph-long stories each day without fail, whether I was 'inspired' or not—particularly if I was not inspired. I was to write without thinking too hard ahead of time about where the story would go, and certainly not thinking ahead to what it would mean—I have never done that. Since I was forcing myself, this produced some curious work: I was allowing my subconscious more of a role than I usually did, and it came out with some interesting themes, subjects, and images. I did not censor what came out, or even revise the paragraph radically—I worked on it only within the bounds of what it had itself established in the way of structure, tone, and imagery. As happens with projects and challenges, after a time I let this one go. By then I had written quite a few of these paragraph stories, sometimes many more than two in one day. And some of them outgrew their paragraphs and developed into longer stories. So the challenge had served its purpose, which was to return me to a good rhythm of productive writing."

ERICA DAWSON was born in 1979 in Columbia, Maryland. After earning her BA in the writing seminars from Johns Hopkins University, she received an MFA in poetry from Ohio State. She is pursuing a PhD in English literature from the University of Cincinnati as the Elliston Fellow in poetry. Her first book of poems, *Big-Eyed Afraid,* winner of the 2006 Anthony Hecht Poetry Prize, was published by Waywiser Press in the United States and in the United Kingdom in 2007.

Dawson writes: "I have always been fascinated by the final line of Wallace Stevens's 'The Snow Man': 'Nothing that is not there and the nothing that is.' When I began thinking about 'Parallax,' I was trying to draw some sort of distinction between perceptions and illusions. I looked at things as understandable as the train barreling past my apartment every two hours and as mind-bending as why the years go fast when their days go slow. With my own lethargy, staring out the window, I remembered a diagram from a grade-school science book illustrating the way your index finger jumps from left to right, moving and not moving, when held in front of your right eye, then left.

"With that illustration in mind, I came up with the refrain and knew I wanted to write a chant royal. I had never done one before and the stanzas' claustrophobia, with the limited rhymes, set inside the expanse of the poem's entire length interested me. I tried to fill the stanzas with things both commonplace (icicles, geese, dreams) and increasingly bizarre in the way they are perceived (the icicles become fingernails, curtains a possible noose). And all the while there's that train. And like the refrain, because of its repetitious appearances, it gains momentum and holds steady, meaning more with each appearance and mattering less, because you've seen it before and you know you will see it again."

CORNELIUS EADY was born in Rochester, New York, in 1954. He is the author of seven books of poetry, including *The Gathering of My Name* (Carnegie Mellon University Press, 1991); *You Don't Miss Your Water* (Henry Holt and Company, 1995); *The Autobiography of a Jukebox* (Carnegie Mellon University Press, 1997); *Brutal Imagination* (G. P. Putnam's Sons, 2001); and *Hardheaded Weather: New and Selected Poems* (Putnam, 2008). He has won a National Endowment for the Arts Fellowship in literature (1985) and a Guggenheim Fellowship in poetry (1993). He is associate professor of English and director of the creative writing program at the University of Notre Dame.

MOIRA EGAN was born in Baltimore, Maryland, in 1962. She studied at Bryn Mawr, Johns Hopkins, and Columbia University, where James Merrill chose her manuscript for the Austin Prize. *Cleave* appeared from Washington Writers' Publishing House (2004). She lives in Rome with her husband, Damiano Abeni.

Of "Millay Goes Down," Egan writes: "These sonnets were written during the sultry summer of 2004, when I had the good fortune to be a Mid-Atlantic Arts Foundation fellow at the Virginia Center for the Creative Arts. Two of my cofellows, Coleman Hough and Erika Meitner, had half-jokingly thrown down a challenge to write a piece about, well, how shall I say it, *le soixante-neuf*. I was reading Edna St. Vincent Millay, whom I've long admired both for her unconventional life and the way she corseted up the details in strict form. So I borrowed that famous first line of hers and, yes indeed, she took me down. I had so much fun with the first that I wrote another. Both quite naughty. But I hope that 'Vincent' would approve."

PETER EVERWINE was born in Detroit, Michigan, in 1930, and raised in western Pennsylvania. Among his books are *Collecting the Animals* (Atheneum, 1973; reprint Carnegie Mellon Classic Contemporary, 2000); *Keeping the Night* (Penumbra Press and Atheneum, 1977); and, most recently, *From the Meadow: Selected and New Poems* (University of Pittsburgh Press, 2004). He has received the Lamont Award and grants from the National Endowment for the Arts and the John Simon Guggenheim Memorial Foundation. He retired from California State University, Fresno, in 1992.

Of "Aubade in Autumn," Everwine writes: "Lawrence and the opening lines of the poem came easily: words out of the blue(s). Then the poem stalled and remained stalled over a long period of time. I didn't want to write a poem about making poems, although the opening lines suggested such a theme. At some later point, I remembered listening to my father sing as he prepared for his mornings. He entered my poem and everything shifted; I had a counter-song where I could listen to his hymn and the undercurrent of blues in the same moment of time. The poem kept turning in unexpected ways, and when I, too, entered its changes, I realized that the poem was truly a love song, with all its attendant joy and sorrow. Auden spoke of being grateful for having written certain poems. For me, 'Aubade in Autumn' is such a poem."

CAROLYN FORCHÉ was born in Detroit in 1950. She is the author of four books of poetry: *Gathering the Tribes,* which received the Yale Younger Poets Award; *The Country Between Us,* chosen as the Lamont Selection of the Academy of American Poets; *The Angel of History,* which won the Los Angeles Times Book Award, and *Blue Hour.* She has translated *Flowers from the Volcano* and *Sorrow* by Claribel Alegría, *Selected Poems of Robert Desnos* (with William Kulik), and Mahmoud Darwish's *Unfortunately, It Was Paradise* (with Munir Akash). She compiled and edited *Against Forgetting: Twentieth-Century Poetry of Witness* (W. W. Norton & Company, 1993). She has received three fellowships from the National Endowment for the Arts, a John Simon Guggenheim Fellowship, and a Lannan Foundation Fellowship. A human rights activist for thirty years, she received the Edita and Ira Morris Hiroshima Foundation Award for Peace and Culture in Stockholm in 1988 for her work on behalf of human rights and the preservation of memory and culture. Forthcoming books include a memoir, *The Horse on Our Balcony* (HarperCollins), a book of essays (HarperCollins), and a fifth collection of poems, *In the Lateness of the World* (HarperCollins). She has taught poetry and literature for thirty-five years and is a member of the faculty of Skidmore College

Forché writes: "'The Museum of Stones' was written, or rather seemed strangely bestowed, in response to the death of a friend who had wandered the world, assembling a collection of stones, bottles of river water, and even bottles of air and smoke as souvenirs of his journeys. He archived the stones meticulously, and while I, too, collected stones for a time, emulating his practice, my curatorial skills were poor, and so rather than a museum, I have several sacks and boxes of stones from special places that can no longer be told apart. The poem began as an elegiac address, and then seemed to pour itself out in a cascade of stone origins and uses. I had a rock collection as a child, so the names of stones entered in, as did the columns and columns of stone in the *Oxford English*. These are some of the sources of 'The Museum of Stones,' though naturally they don't account for what the poem became in its writing."

CHRIS FORHAN was born in Seattle, Washington, in 1959. His two books of poetry are *The Actual Moon, The Actual Stars* (Northeastern University Press, 2003), which won the Morse Poetry Prize and a Washington State Book Award, and *Forgive Us Our Happiness* (University Press of New England, 1999), which won the Bakeless Prize. He has received a National Endowment for the Arts Fellowship. He teaches at Butler University in Indianapolis.

Of "Rock Polisher," Forhan writes: "When I was growing up, a neighbor family owned a rock polisher—a machine that enchanted us by slowly, over several days, smoothing a small stone, making it pretty enough to display on a shelf. In retrospect, this practice strikes me as poignantly beside the point, as if, rock by rock, we would make nature more to our liking. It is also a tempting metaphor; thus, the poem, the writing of which provided me no small delight as I followed the conceit to its logical (or illogical) conclusion. I also enjoyed giving myself permission to engage in manic, sometimes clunky sound work, which I hope underscores the poem's sense of hopeful fumbling. Regardless, sonic hijinks are something for which I have a high tolerance."

JOHN GALLAHER was born in Portland, Oregon, in 1965. He lived in several states while growing up, finally attending Texas State University and Ohio University. His books of poetry are *Gentlemen in Turbans, Ladies in Cauls* (Spuyten Duyvil, 2001), *The Little Book of Guesses* (Four Way Books, Levis Poetry Prize, 2007), and *Radio Good Luck* (Four Way Books, forthcoming). He lives in rural Missouri with his family, where he teaches and coedits *The Laurel Review*.

Of "In the Book of the Disappearing Book," Gallaher writes: "Several years ago I was riding on a train. I remember nothing about the trip (which might have been around Baltimore), other than the fact that I was struck by the image of a woman reading a book across the aisle, the way her dress disappeared in her reflection in the window, causing it to seem as if her head and hands were floating disembodied through the landscape. I spent the trip mesmerized by the blur of it. Having no one there with me whom I could tap and say 'look,' I just had to sit there quietly. Therefore, the poem. And then the fact that I've often felt that I'm on some train somewhere, wanting to say something to some absent someone."

JAMES GALVIN was born in Chicago, Illinois, in 1951. He teaches at the Iowa Writers' Workshop. His books are *Imaginary Timber* (1980), *God's Mistress* (1984), *Elements* (1988), and *Lethal Frequencies* (1995), all collected in *Resurrection Update*, 1997, from Copper Canyon Press. Copper Canyon also published *X* in 2003. Galvin has published two prose works, *The Meadow* and *Fencing the Sky*, both from Henry Holt and Company. He has just finished a new book of poems.

Of "Girl without Her Nightgown" Galvin writes: "Hurricane Katrina has, like so many recent historical events, a quality of allegorical nonfiction about it. She was, for example, her own prophecy, as she pirouetted slowly in the Gulf, telegraphing her landfall, which the government ignored. Then there is the personal loss and suffering of the victims and refugees, which continues today, perhaps because it is usurped in our consciousness by other, more recent historical allegories. Then there is the allegory of our moral disarray as a society, and the allegory of our mortal existence on earth, both as present and as prophecy.

"I happened, also, to be thinking about refrains. What makes a merely annoying repetition as opposed to a killer refrain? 'With hey, ho, the wind and the rain.'"

LOUISE GLÜCK was born in New York City in 1943. She is the author of eleven books of poetry, including, most recently, *Averno* (Farrar, Straus, and Giroux, 2006). She has won the Pulitzer Prize, the Bollingen Prize, and the National Book Critics Circle Award. She has also published a collection of essays, *Proofs and Theories: Essays on Poetry* (Ecco Press, 1994). She now teaches at Yale University and since 2003 has served as judge of the Yale Series of Younger Poets. She lives in Cambridge, Mass-achusetts. She was guest editor of *The Best American Poetry 1993*.

Glück says: "I prefer that the reader make his or her own discoveries undirected by the poet. 'Threshing' is part of a new book."

JORIE GRAHAM was born in New York City in 1950. Her books include *The Dream of the Unified World: Selected Poems 1974–1994* (1995), *Never* (2002), and *Overlord* (2005), all from Ecco Press. She taught at the Iowa Writers' Workshop for many years and was the guest editor of *The Best American Poetry 1990*. She received the 1996 Pulitzer Prize in poetry. She succeeded Seamus Heaney as the Boylston Professor of Rhetoric at Harvard University.

ROBERT HASS was born in San Francisco in 1941. He teaches at the University of California at Berkeley. His most recent book is *Time and Materials* (Ecco Press), winner of the 2007 National Book Award. A collection of columns written for *The Washington Post* was published as *Now & Then: The Poet's Choice Columns, 1997–2000* (Shoemaker & Hoard). He was the guest editor of *The Best American Poetry 2001*.

Of "I Am Your Waiter Tonight and My Name Is Dmitri," Hass writes: "I think this poem came out of rereading *Crime and Punishment* at a time when I was also thinking about the violence of the twentieth century and our invasion of Iraq. And thinking about John Ashbery and poetry and war and honey."

BOB HICOK was born in Grand Ledge, Michigan, in 1960. He teaches creative writing at Virginia Tech University. *This Clumsy Living*, his fifth book, was published by the University of Pittsburgh Press in 2007.

Of "O my pa-pa," Hicok writes: "About this poem I have little to say. I'm happy it's here and will share that it has been admired by some and attacked by others, in the small ways of aesthetic love and hate among poets. Having published poems markedly different in the same year, and finding myself a housemate if not bedfellow to poets of a different stripe—poets who crave or despise closure, who depend on or deny the ability of language to convey any or explicit meaning—I want to say, more than anything, that there is no type of poem we need more than another. For poets, this back section of *The Best American Poetry* is one of the most interesting spaces in American letters. We're asked to talk about poems that will soon be praised or scorned based largely on their inclusion in this volume. I thought, in this context, I might declare where I stand. So: I enjoy narrative and surreal poems, lyric poems and prose poems. The elliptical poets, of all the geometrically named poets, have the coolest images and the most assistant professorships. The objectivists—are they still out there? I hope so. George Oppen, we miss you. As someone not me says, 'It's all good.' I think what I really wanted to say is let's stop picking on the Language Poets. Ron Silliman, you silly man, let's do the cheer together: give me an L, an A, etcetera. What's that spell? Laetcetera."

BRENDA HILLMAN was born in Tucson, Arizona, in 1951. She was educated at Pomona College and received her MFA at the University of Iowa. Her books include *Pieces of Air in the Epic* (Wesleyan University Press, 2005), *Cascadia* (2001), *Loose Sugar* (1997), *Bright Existence* (1993), and *White Dress* (1985). She has edited an edition of Emily Dickinson's poetry for Shambhala Publications. She is on the faculty of Saint Mary's College in Moraga, California, where she is the Olivia C. Filippi Professor of Poetry. She is involved with anti-war activism as a member of the CODEPINK in the San Francisco Bay Area.

Hillman writes: "'Phone Booth' accretes lines that might be thought of as independent smaller poems. I'd drafted it in much longer form (at Squaw Valley Community). It derives from certain ideas about emotion. I'm interested in feeling-seeds for lyric collage that are hybrids— like sadness that is full of bemusement or dread-excitement, etc., in this case a mix of Gnostic sorrow/empathy for obsolescent things like the noble, retired phone booths and aspects of expression like the interpunct, plus a hatred of soulless fetishized objects (cell phones) and a firm and permanent adoration of Rimbaud."

TONY HOAGLAND was born in Tucson, Arizona, in 1953. He won the Poetry Foundation's 2005 Mark Twain Award for humor in American poetry. His books of poems include *What Narcissism Means to Me* (Graywolf Press, 2003), *Donkey Gospel* (Graywolf, 1998), and *Hard Rain* (Hollyridge Press, 2005). *Real Sofistikashun,* a collection of essays, was published by Graywolf in 2006. He has received grants from the National Endowment for the Arts and the Guggenheim Foundation. He teaches at the University of Houston and in the Warren Wilson MFA program.

Of "Muchness," Hoagland writes: "While on a walk, a friend of mine once said to me, 'Surely, in the history of humankind, there have been as many poems written about happiness as unhappiness.' Then, after a minute of thought, we both burst into laughter. Misfortune, misery, and dissatisfied desire (a more privileged illness) are strong motivations for the making, shaping act of art. Like a stone tossed into a pond, affliction throws off ripples of narrative.

"But the condition of fullness doesn't demand analysis or articulation in the way a wound does, doesn't demand *transformation*. Yet in our sullen juju-art, it would seem wise to acknowledge and encourage good fortune, too. The day I wrote much of 'Muchness,' I was happy to see my loved one go away for the day. After the boat she was on disappeared, the landscape—green Argentina—shimmered crisper. The thick jungle and blue-gray sea, which had been displaced by the static of people-presence, came back, greener and bluer than ever. I accidentally became conscious that description, a truly peaceful and useless enterprise, fulfills another kind of need."

GARRETT HONGO was born in Volcano, Hawai'i, in 1951 and grew up on the North Shore of O'ahu and in Los Angeles. His work includes two books of poetry, three anthologies, and *Volcano: A Memoir of Hawai'i*. He has received a Guggenheim Fellowship, two National Endowment for the Arts grants, and the Lamont Poetry Prize from the Academy of American Poets. He teaches at the University of Oregon, where he is Distinguished Professor of Arts and Sciences.

Of "Cane Fire," Hongo writes: "The poem grows out of family stories—or a narrative quilt I made of some scraps of stories. The main one— about the murder-suicide and the cane fire—I got from my maternal great-aunts (my grandmother's two younger sisters), who were great storytellers. The adoption tale my grandmother told me herself. They've stayed in my mind for about thirty years now, and I've just tried to weave a whole book out of them about the sugar plantation, the village there, and my family history on the North Shore of O'ahu. It's also about my own love of that landscape and what it means to me—that it's not 'Margaritaville' or anything like that, but full of Gothic markers to the past, really, amidst all the beauty and lavishness. It's tough *and* it's beautiful."

RICHARD HOWARD was born in Cleveland, Ohio, in 1929. He teaches in the writing division of Columbia University's School of the Arts, and continues against all odds to translate works of literature from the

French. The most recent of his fifteen books of poems, *Without Saying,* was published in 2008 by Turtle Point Press. He was the guest editor of *The Best American Poetry 1995.*

Of "The Rape of the Daughters of Leucippus by Castor and Pollux," Howard writes: "The poem, composed in reverent yet delighted recognition of Rubens's mastery of the hard truths that underlie soft legends, is a sort of apology for Received Standard Versions of the old outrages. I find myself recurring to the lovable and (therefore?) much-abused figure of Leda in poem after poem I write or at least want to write; surely Yeats and Mona van Duyn *need not* have had the Last Word."

MARK JARMAN was born in Mount Sterling, Kentucky, in 1952. His nine books of poetry include *North Sea* (Cleveland State University Poetry Center, 1978), *Far and Away* (Carnegie Mellon University Press, 1985), *The Black Riviera* (Wesleyan University Press, 1990), *Questions for Ecclesiastes* (Story Line Press, 1997), *Unholy Sonnets* (Story Line Press, 2000), *To the Green Man* (Sarabande Books, 2004), and *Epistles* (Sarabande, 2007). *Questions for Ecclesiastes* won the 1998 Lenore Marshal Poetry Prize from the Academy of American Poets and *The Nation* magazine. He has written two collections of essays and reviews, *The Secret of Poetry* (Story Line, 2001) and *Body and Soul: Essays on Poetry* (University of Michigan Press, 2002). He is Centennial Professor of English at Vanderbilt University in Nashville, Tennessee.

Jarman writes: "For years I had cherished the experience described in 'Snoring,' occasionally sharing it with friends, but was never able to write about it. Finally, when a friend explained what probably happened, how I had not discovered a telepathic, spiritual bond with my father but rather had affected the environment in the room just by waking up to his snoring, I was at last able to write the poem. The word emerges when the experience is broken open. Bad for the experience, perhaps, but good for the poem."

GEORGE KALAMARAS was born in Chicago, Illinois, in 1956. He is the author of six books of poetry, the most recent being *Gold Carp Jack Fruit Mirrors* (The Bitter Oleander Press, 2008) and *Even the Java Sparrows Call Your Hair* (Quale Press, 2004). His work has appeared previously in *The Best American Poetry 1997.* He has received fellowships from the National Endowment for the Arts (1993) and the Indiana Arts Commission (2001), and first prize in the 1998 *Abiko Quarterly* International Poetry Prize (Japan). He is also the author of a 1994 scholarly book on Hindu mysticism and Western language theory, *Reclaiming the Tacit Dimension: Symbolic Form in the Rhetoric of Silence* (State University of New York Press). He is professor of English at Indiana University–Purdue University in Fort Wayne, where he has taught since 1990.

Of "Francis Ponge Is on Fire," Kalamaras writes: "I have long admired the work of the French writer Francis Ponge (1899–1988), whose experiments with form helped foster a new avenue in world poetry, particularly blurred-genre work. One remarkable thing about Ponge's prose poems (which investigate everything from 'The Delights of the Door' to 'The Oyster') is that they are always understated, almost 'scientific' in their reach toward the recording of observations of both the human and, in particular, the natural world. An interesting transparency often occurs in his work between the outer world and the psyche of the writer, as well as, in turn, the psyche of the reader—something Robert Bly might call 'poems of twofold consciousness.' The prose poem of mine included here attempts both to honor Ponge's enormous contribution and to extend the reach of this transparency, moving it further into areas of the surreal."

MARY KARR was born in southeast Texas in 1955. Her most recent poetry collection is *Sinners Welcome* (HarperCollins). *LIT,* her third memoir, will appear next year from the same publisher. She now writes the "Poet's Choice" column for *The Washington Post Book World.*

Of "Recuperation from the Dead Love through Christ and Isaac Babel," Karr writes: "When a romance of mine ended brutally, I found myself a disillusioned Christian in New York's Hell's Kitchen, sleeplessly reading Isaac Babel's *Red Calvary* stories, which recount his service as a propagandist in a bloodied Russian army that would—under Stalin—wind up killing him. One of the most riveting stories, 'Konkin,' begins, 'So there we were making mincemeat of the Poles. So much so that the trees were rattling. I'd been hit in the morning but managed to keep buzzing more or less. . . . All around me everyone's hugging each other with hatchets, like priests from two villages, the sap's slowly trickling out of me, my horse has pissed all over itself. Need I say more?' At dawn, I set out to mail my ex-fiancé's parcel back, and I found—through prayer and meditation on Babel's own tragedy—something worthy of worship in the carnivalesque streetscape outside my door."

MAXINE KUMIN was born in Philadelphia, Pennsylvania, in 1925. She is the author of sixteen books of poetry, the most recent of which, *Still to*

Mow (W. W. Norton & Company), appeared in 2007. The first, *Halfway*, was published in 1961; the fourth, *Up Country*, won the Pulitzer Prize in 1973. *Looking for Luck* won the Poets' Prize in 1994. In 1976, Kumin and her husband moved to a derelict farm in central New Hampshire. Here, they raised horses, composted the manure to fertilize their vegetable garden, turned two former gravel pits into wildlife habitats, worked with the Forest Society to manage two hundred acres of mixed timber, and continue to take in a succession of shelter dogs.

Of "Though He Tarry," Kumin writes: "Although, or maybe especially because, I am a nonbeliever, I am deeply touched by the eternal longing for a messiah. I don't know where I read the line attributed to Maimonides or the other data cited in the poem, but I'm a compulsive jotter down of intriguing quotes and statistics, which usually come to no good end. But once in a while, a poem breaks through."

ADRIE KUSSEROW was born in Underhill, Vermont, in 1966. At nineteen, she traveled to Kathmandu, Nepal, and Dharamsala, India (home of the Tibetan government in exile), where she studied Tibetan Buddhism. She chairs the department of sociology and anthropology at St. Michael's College in Colchester, Vermont. She lives on the land she grew up on, with her mother, husband, and two children, Ana and Willem. She has been to refugee camps in Kathmandu, Nepal; Dharamsala, India; and northern Uganda. She and her husband now work with Sudanese refugees in building schools in South Sudan with the New Sudan Education Initiative, www.nesei.org. Her first book of poems, *Hunting Down the Monk*, was published by BOA Editions, Ltd. (2002), and her first work of ethnography, *American Individualisms*, appeared from Palgrave Macmillan (2004).

Of "Skull Trees, South Sudan," Kusserow writes: "I wrote this poem after returning from a service learning trip in which my husband and I took St. Michael's College students to a Sudanese refugee camp in northern Uganda. We decided to take students to northern Uganda when one of the Lost Boys of Sudan we are very close to, Atem Deng, found out his father was alive."

ALEX LEMON was born in Osage, Iowa, in 1978. He was educated at Macalester College and the University of Minnesota. He is the author of *Mosquito* (Tin House Books, 2006) and *Hallelujah Blackout* (Milkweed Editions, 2008). In 2005 he was awarded a fellowship from the National Endowment for the Arts and a grant from the Minnesota Arts Board. He enjoys tending to tomatoes and kale. He is grateful and forever listening.

Lemon writes: "The germ for this excerpt from 'Hallelujah Blackout' began in a conversation with Ryan Black on the Washington Avenue Bridge in Minneapolis, Minnesota, in 2001. We were watching the barges below as we walked to class at the university. Ryan shook his head and said that Minnesota had 'too many bridges . . . too many.' We laughed, and the cold air made us look like we'd been eating fire. That night I put on a very small, very tight, bright red snowmobile suit and wore it around for several days. Late in the summer of 2007 I walked across the same bridge listening to a song by Okkervil River and humming."

PHILIP LEVINE was born in Detroit, Michigan, in 1928. He now lives half the year in Fresno, California, and half in Brooklyn. His most recent books are *Breath* (Alfred A. Knopf, 2004) and *Tarumba* (Sarabande Books, 2007), the selected poems of the great Mexican poet Jaime Sabines, translated by Levine and the late Mexican poet Ernesto Trejo.

Of "Of Love and Other Disasters," Levine writes: "Ten years ago a friend showed me a manuscript, a collection of poems—dramatic monologues—the working title of which was something like 'Lectures on Love.' I told him to change the title because no one likes to be lectured and as far as I could tell he didn't know any more about love than I did, & I knew almost nothing. I suggested he use the title 'Of Love and Other Disasters.' He dropped the original title but did not take my suggestion. So my brilliant title lay smothering in the foul air of memory until a year or so ago when suddenly I recalled a foreman I'd worked under back in 1952 in a machine shop near Tiger Stadium. I'll call him Conroy—he was Irish—a big, awkward man, essentially friendly but with no gift for making friends. Conroy, recently divorced, was obsessed with his loneliness, with the absence of women from his life. Once I quit the job and stopped going to O'Neil's, the neighborhood bar, I lost contact with Conroy. What would have happened to him—I wondered—if he'd met the one woman in the world who could abide his fumbling needs? Would he manage to step on her foot or would he turn & run?"

J. D. MCCLATCHY was born in Bryn Mawr, Pennsylvania, in 1945. A new book of poems, *Mercury Dressing,* will be published by Knopf next year. In 2008, his edition of Hugo von Hofmannsthal's selected writings, called *A World of Difference,* will appear from Princeton University Press, and an anthology of poems, *The Four Seasons,* from Everyman's Library. New operas have been appearing: an English version of *The Magic Flute* at the Met last year; coming soon, *Little Nemo* with music by Ned

Rorem and *The Secret Agent* with music by Michael Dellaira. He is the editor of *The Yale Review*.

Of "Resignation," McClatchy writes: "It was an odd collision—coming across the line by Willa Cather at the same time I was brooding on love's helplessness. Why is it that the most powerful feeling in our lives is so easily betrayed and shattered? Cather's remark suddenly gave moral weight to the other pan on the scale, and tipped me toward the poem. I had gone to a concert of Britten cantatas that night, but couldn't get the Cather line out of my mind the whole time I sat there. I came home and wrote the poem out in fifteen minutes. When I finished, I felt the little thing had taken a lifetime."

DAVIS McCOMBS was born in Louisville, Kentucky, in 1969. He attended Harvard University, the University of Virginia, and Stanford University as a Wallace Stegner Fellow in poetry. His first book, *Ultima Thule*, was chosen by W. S. Merwin as the 1999 volume in the Yale Series of Younger Poets. Linda Gregerson selected his second book, *Dismal Rock* (Tupelo Press, 2007), for the 2005 Dorset Prize. He directs the creative writing program at the University of Arkansas.

McCombs writes: "Dismal Rock is a cracked sandstone bluff rising over two hundred feet above the east bank of the Nolin River in Edmonson County, Kentucky. Near its base, on January 16, 1902, a man named Noah Duvall shot and killed the last gray wolf in Edmonson County. The story, first told to me by my friend Mark Willis, combines so many of the elements I'm interested in: local history, extinction, the fraught line where agriculture and nature meet, our changing attitudes toward the natural world, the fairy-tale associations of wolves, even the biblical echo of the name Noah. I knew immediately I had to write about it."

W. S. MERWIN was born in New York City in 1927. He was educated at Princeton. From 1949 to 1951 he worked as a tutor in France, Portugal, and Majorca, later earning his living by translating from the French, Spanish, Latin, and Portuguese. About those early years, Merwin told Ben George of *Fugue* magazine that he "mainly had a hand-to-mouth existence for years. I worked as a tutor, and you didn't make much money doing that. Then I went to England and I lived on what I earned from the BBC, which wasn't very much, but enough to manage to live. It didn't take much money. So I just kept that going as long as I could. I kept thinking, *It'll come to an end and I'll have to go to a university.* But year after year it didn't. And then I got a few fellowships. . . . My models were people who lived on very little money, who assumed that if you were a writer or a composer or something like that you didn't have much money. Maybe later on in your life you had a bit. But you took it for granted that you'd have no money. It didn't seem important." *A Mask for Janus,* Merwin's first book of poems, was chosen by W. H. Auden as the 1952 volume in the Yale Series of Younger Poets. Recent collections include *Present Company* (Copper Canyon Press, 2007); *Migration: New & Selected Poems* (2005), which won the 2005 National Book Award; and *The Pupil* (2002). His new book is *The Shadow of Sirius* (Copper Canyon Press, 2008). He lives in Haiku, Hawaii.

Of "A Letter to Su Tung P'o," Merwin writes: "It seems as though I have been sending a letter to Su Tung P'o for most of my life. The great poets of the Chinese Tang and Song dynasties, as their poems have reached us through the translations of Arthur Waley and others, wrote with an apparent intimacy that altered the whole sound of poetry in English for the past hundred years. It was Burton Watson's translations of Su Tung P'o that made the voice of that poet seem clearest to me. Some of his versions have haunted me for decades. One of those is a night piece, a river poem, the words speaking, or singing, from a boat moored on a long journey, before daybreak. It evokes a moment of great stillness and distance, and of evanescence before departure. After reading the poem many times through the years, I read it again late one night in the house where I live, on the side of a wooded valley that is still blessed at night with its own deep silence, and I found myself beginning to answer the ancient poet."

SUSAN MITCHELL was born in 1944, grew up in New York City, and was educated at Wellesley College, Georgetown University, and Columbia University. Her most recent book of poems is *Erotikon* (HarperCollins, 2000). Her previous book, *Rapture* (HarperCollins, 1992), won the Kingsley Tufts Poetry Award. She has received fellowships from the Guggenheim Foundation, the Lannan Foundation, and the National Endowment for the Arts. She is a professor in the graduate creative writing program at Florida Atlantic University and divides her time between Boca Raton, Florida, and Washington, Connecticut

Of "Ritual," Mitchell writes: "Near my house is an abandoned estate where I sometimes go to think and dream. The property, with its tangle of trees and vines and overgrown walkways, extends to the Intracoastal, and there at the water's edge in the shade of three mangroves, their roots home to tiny oysters and crabs, I have a simple lunch of bread, cheese, and wine. These lunches always end the same way: I throw the remaining scraps of bread to the silty current. The first time I threw it was to see what, if anything, lived in those waters. But now I throw to see the water leap up and hurl itself onto the bread. Whatever is down there, it is always too quick for me; I have never seen it.

"'Ritual' began for me the day I all at once saw my gesture from outside and felt my bread-throwing charged with symbolic meaning."

PAUL MULDOON was born in 1951 in County Armagh, Northern Ireland, and was educated in Armagh and at the Queen's University of Belfast. From 1973 to 1986 he worked in Belfast as a radio and television producer for the British Broadcasting Corporation. Since 1987 he has lived in the United States, where he is now Howard G. B. Clark '21 Professor in the Humanities at Princeton University. Between 1999 and 2004 he was Professor of Poetry at the University of Oxford. His most recent collections of poetry include *Hay* (1998), *Poems 1968–1998* (2001), the Pulitzer Prize–winning *Moy Sand and Gravel* (2002), and *Horse Latitudes* (2006), all from Farrar, Straus and Giroux. He was the guest editor of *The Best American Poetry 2005*. In 2007 he was appointed poetry editor of *The New Yorker*.

Muldoon writes: "The water cooler of the title is a modern version of the parish pump, where tittle-tattle and tall tales are the order of the day. Something of the fallout of the office Christmas party is hinted at there in 'the mistletoe puts up its mitts,' while the notion of 'trying to get something clear' is probably the last thing on the minds of anyone in the poem, including the oddly hesitant speaker, whose little two-steps-forward-one-step-back is somehow in sync with the verse form of the poem—the pantoum. The idea of the metaphorically poisonous tongue is made literal here, since modern scientists have concluded that trees are actually attempting to kill off their neighbors by releasing acids into the air and earth. It's a turf war, alright, down by the water cooler—the black oaks, the chestnuts, and the maples being the most bloody-minded of all."

D. NURKSE was born in New York City in 1949 and currently teaches at Sarah Lawrence College. He is the author of nine books of poetry, including *The Border Kingdom, Burnt Island,* and *The Fall* (Knopf, 2008, 2005, and 2002). He received a 2007 Guggenheim Fellowship. He has taught in the Stonecoast MFA program, the Brooklyn College MFA program, The New School, Rikers's Island Correctional Facility, and in inner-city literacy programs.

Of "The Gate of Abraham," Nurkse writes: "My poem is very directly inspired by Jean de Joinville's account of the seventh crusade in 1244, when the European 'appetite for reality' led deeper and deeper into a dreamworld of bloodshed and surreal realignments. Joinville was close to King Louis during the failure of that mission, but he refused to participate in the next war. I've always been astonished at the older woman who strides in and out of the story, without explanation, ready to destroy heaven and hell (and convinced that it is possible to do so). She reminds me of my late friend Grace Paley."

DEBRA NYSTROM was born in Pierre, South Dakota, in 1954, and teaches now in the creative writing program at the University of Virginia. She is the author of *A Quarter Turn* (Sheep Meadow Press, 1991), *Torn Sky* (Sarabande Books, 2003), and *Bad River Road,* which will be published by Sarabande Books in 2009. She lives with her husband, Dan O'Neill, and their daughter, Mia, in Charlottesville, Virginia.

Nystrom writes: "'Every Night' began as notes for my brother and his lawyer, words and phrases jotted down after phone calls and visits during the nine months my brother was in custody before sentencing. Like most of the people he met in that time, my brother had been arrested for drugs, and had had, in his strung-out state of denial beforehand, little sense of the complex stakes involved. Over those months, I heard bits about other guys who came through as prisoners—not stories about crimes, but echoes of confinement. When I went to see him, there were always delays, and sometimes I talked with family members of other men there, especially in the close quarters at the county jail where this poem is set. Visitors never heard a thing from the jail's two crowded cells, but I know I wasn't the only one sitting on the benches outside, recalling sounds and images I had been told about in calls from within. There are more severe places to be held, though Hughes County Jail exemplifies conditions and habeas corpus problems present in many parts of our country. The poem is mostly about listening, I think—and about loss, which may be the original, inscrutable cause of most actions that land people in jail or prison. Loss, in any case, seems to be the overwhelming experience Inside. The names in 'Every Night' are invented, and the poem's central speaker is not my brother, but the voices are meant to be true to those who have passed through that place—and to my brother, whose work now involves a great deal of listening."

MEGHAN O'ROURKE was born in New York City in 1976. She is the literary editor of *Slate Magazine* and poetry coeditor of *The Paris Review.* Her first book of poems, *Halflife*, was published by W. W. Norton & Company in 2007. She received the 2005 Union League Civic and Arts Foundation Award for poetry.

O'Rourke writes: "'The Window at Arles' was an attempt to investigate the proximity between creation and destruction. It was also originally part of a larger series that interwove fragments of biographical material (letters, diaries) with imagined situations; the aim was to exploit the gap between what was 'real' and what was patently invented, and, in fragmenting what might otherwise be a narrative account of 'making,' to examine, somehow, the failure of language (or any form of representation) to communicate without slippage. The evolving quotation (which begins as Van Gogh's language and then morphs into something else) was meant to provide a destabilizing friction, one that would call into question the integrity of the whole."

Ron Padgett was born in Tulsa, Oklahoma, in 1942. His most recent collection of poems is *How to Be Perfect* (Coffee House Press, 2007). Other books include *You Never Know* (Coffee House, 2002), *If I Were You* (Proper Tales Press, 2007), and *Joe: A Memoir of Joe Brainard* (Coffee House, 2004). Padgett's translations include Blaise Cendrars's *Complete Poems* (University of California Press, 1992), Pierre Reverdy's *Prose Poems* (Black Square Editions/The Brooklyn Rail, 2007) and, with Bill Zavatsky, Valery Larbaud's *Poems of A. O. Barnabooth* (Black Widow Press, 2008).

Of "Method, or Kenneth Koch," Padgett writes: "My poem grew out of my thinking about a dishwashing soap that I had discovered a few years ago in a supermarket, a nicely colored liquid in a curvy bottle with an unusually abstract name—Method—which I associated with Descartes's *Discourse on Method*. At that time I was pondering the introduction I was writing for the Library of America edition of Kenneth Koch's *Selected Poems*. The confluence of discovery, the soap itself, Descartes, and Kenneth seems to have made me want to write."

Michael Palmer was born in Manhattan in 1943 and has lived in San Francisco since 1969. He has worked with the Margaret Jenkins Dance Company for more than thirty years. His most recent collections are *At Passages* (1995), *The Lion Bridge: Selected Poems 1972–1995* (1998), *The Promises of Glass* (2000), *Codes Appearing: Poems 1979–1988* (2001), and *Company of Moths* (2005), all from New Directions. He won the 2006 Wallace Stevens Award from the Academy of American Poets.

Of "The Classical Study (4)," Palmer writes: "The Master (full title: Master of Shadows) arrives unpredictably, perhaps elicited by questions I'm in the midst of formulating for him. He may appear while I'm walking by the sea, or while I'm touring the commercial district of downtown Kyoto or, as here, while I'm wandering the somewhat forlorn streets of central Rochester during a brief visit to the University of Rochester. Frequently inebriated and disoriented, he evades my questions as best he can. This is the source of his wisdom."

D. A. POWELL was born in Albany, Georgia, in 1963. His books include *Tea* (Wesleyan University Press, 1998), *Lunch* (Wesleyan, 2000), and *Cocktails* (Graywolf, 2004). He has taught at Columbia University, University of Iowa, San Francisco State University, and Harvard University. He is now on the English faculty at the University of San Francisco.

Of "cosmos, late blooming," Powell writes: "I've never much been a fan of cultivated flowers. Gladiolas remind me of funerals, roses remind me of weddings, carnations remind me of high school dances: in short, the associations I make with such flowers are entirely negative. But the wildflowers, the ones that seem to thrive in the most inhospitable places, fascinate me. I admire cosmos because it grows in the margins and interstices, where the more delicate plants would die for lack of nutrients. As we overload the environment with pollution, isn't it amazing that something beautiful can endure in spite of us? I find it a source of great hope that, when everything else has begun to die and fall away, there might still be a blossom opening somewhere."

ALBERTO RÍOS was born in Nogales, Arizona, in 1952. His nine collections of poetry include *The Smallest Muscle in the Human Body* (2002) and *The Theater of Night* (2006), both from Copper Canyon. He has also written three short story collections and a memoir, *Capirotada,* about growing up on the Mexican border. Regent's Professor and the Katharine C. Turner Chair in English, he has taught at Arizona State University for more than twenty-five years.

Of "The Rain That Falls Here," Ríos writes: "Every several years, the weather on Southern California's coast gets extreme and in its frenzy ends up disorienting all kinds of animals, particularly birds, sometimes pelicans, forcefully driving them off course so much that they land badly in Arizona's desert, occasionally reaching Phoenix. They're exhausted and upset, and sometimes find themselves pacing on freeway medians, overwhelmed by the traffic and the strangeness of it all, the wind from the cars not quite the wind from the ocean, but close enough to keep them confused.

"This poem stemmed from a recent such incident, when I saw a very upset pelican myself. Along with thinking about how to help, it made me curious about what else might be mixed up, what might be similarly disoriented, and thinking about water itself in the desert.

"Water, of course, is that same stranger to Arizona, a visitor that must be reintroduced to this place every time, and which behaves so erratically that it seems as confused as the pelican. With that, the poem began."

TIM ROSS was born in Newark, Ohio, in 1976. He currently lives in Nashville, where he teaches at Belmont University and Tennessee State University. He has received two fellowships from the Fine Arts Work Center in Provincetown.

Of "then let fall your horrible pleasure," Ross writes: "I wrote this poem while I was reading a handful of popular books on modern physics, specifically relativity, quantum mechanics, and string theory. These were books for a general audience—Stephen Hawking's *The Theory of Everything,* Brian Greene's *The Elegant Universe,* and a few others—physics without the math, which my mathematician friend tells me isn't physics. My knowledge or understanding of the field is cursory at best, but I was interested in the ongoing attempt to describe the structure of the universe. The title of the poem is quoted from *King Lear,* act three, scene two, where Lear is out in the woods shaking his fist at the heavens, which maybe suggests the odd combination of nobility and absurdity in the activity of the scientists about which I was reading. In the poem, the physicist is a religious ascetic, a hermit, an outcast, a reviled creature, and an artist."

JOHN RYBICKI was born in Detroit, Michigan, in 1961, grew up there, and is currently writer-in-residence at Alma College. He also works with Wings of Hope Hospice, teaching poetry writing to children who have gone through a trauma or loss. He is the author of three books of poems: *Traveling at High Speeds* (New Issues Poetry & Prose), *Yellow-Haired Girl with Spider* (March Street Press, 2002), and his latest collection, *We Bed Down into Water,* which is now available from Northwestern University Press.

Of "Three Lanterns," Rybicki writes: "I used to do yearlong residencies teaching creative writing to inner-city children in Detroit. All year those students poured their fire over me like holy water. It helped fill a colossal hole in me: I ached for fatherhood so desperately it felt like I had a sky in me holding its breath. Because of years of chemotherapy (my wife has non-Hodgkin's lymphoma), we were not able to have children. When summer came and the kids disappeared, I felt desolation.

"The summer of 2003, I became a Big Brother to Martel Epperson, a young seer in one of my writing classes who lived in the marrow of Detroit. We'd meet once a week and hoof across the grass tossing the football, then we'd go out on my dad's boat. At sundown, we'd write about our adventures in a memory book. At the end of the summer, my wife, my brother Benny, and I took Martel to Cedar Point Amusement Park. When we brought him home in the dark, we found glass shattered everywhere and bullet holes in the front door to his house. Through this violent sort of providence, Martel Epperson, a soldier at thirteen, came to be our son.

"We swaddled Martel in our covered wagon and smuggled him out to the land of the leaping frogs and sandhill cranes. The first year Martel came to live with us, my wife's cancer came back and she was living 'on the floor / where the fish were frying,' as a result of the latest in a long line of treatments for her disease.

"I can't use a hammer and chisel to fix the broken parts of my wife or son, but on the page anything is possible. Poetry allows me to trump human limitation and enact the kind of healing I can't achieve in the literal world."

IRA SADOFF was born in Brooklyn, New York, in 1945. His books include *Barter* (University of Illinois Press, 2003), *Grazing* (University of Illinois Press, 1998), *An Ira Sadoff Reader* (University of New England Press/Bread Loaf, 1992), *Settling Down* (Houghton Mifflin, 1975), and a forthcoming book of literary criticism, *In the Margins* (University of Iowa Press, 2009). He teaches at Colby College in Maine.

Sadoff writes: "'American' resembles some of my earlier poems, poems that are drawn to a subject and a memory, also in the way I had become suspicious of lyric 'I' poems as self-aggrandizing, or as losing a sense of scope and scale. So in this poem I pressurized the narrative elements and the jagged music of the poem as much as felt authentic, then I asked the question I ask of most of my poems now, which is 'what's next?' Memory, story, and self most often don't suffice to make a poem with vision, so I began looking for correspondences, differences, how I could make the experience larger with metaphor, how I could take the too easy gloss of the embarrassment and self-absorption of a young person to a more difficult place. It's not easy to romanticize Archie Shepp: in his later years he often used drink and his instrument to express his bitterness and disappointment, his diminishment as a man. As a member of the audience, as he stared at us, I think I knew something about how he felt, what many of us sometimes feel like as 'Americans' now with diminished agency and idealism."

DAVID ST. JOHN was born in Fresno, California, in 1949. He is the author of nine collections of poetry, most recently *The Face: A Novella in Verse* (HarperCollins, 2004). He teaches in the PhD program in literature and creative writing at the University of Southern California.

St. John writes: "In 'The Aurora of the New Mind,' I was hoping to mix a variety of tonalities and temporalities, then shake them (not stirred, but stirring) like a martini until the icy dryness, or dry icyness, of the poem came clear."

SHEROD SANTOS was born in Greenville, South Carolina, in 1948. He is the author of five books of poetry, including, most recently, *The Perishing* (W. W. Norton & Company, 2003). In 2005 he published *Greek Lyric Poetry: A New Translation* (Norton), and in 2000 a collection of literary essays, *A Poetry of Two Minds* (University of Georgia Press). He received an Award for Literary Excellence from the American Academy of Arts and Letters in 1999. He lives in Chicago, where he is finishing a play called *The Flaying of Marsyas*.

Santos writes: "As the epigraph notes, 'World News' is an 'account' of Baudelaire's 'Le Voyage,' so it's not to be confused with translation, nor even with any of the various forms of literary adaptation. What it is is something that felt, in the writing, more like a waking dream of the original, the cultural and spiritual malaise of Baudelaire's nineteenth-century Paris irrupting into the chronicles of the present day. The degree to which his poems foresaw the tragic nature of the modern world may explain both his personal torment and his visionary reach; certainly it was his special genius to recognize how the particulars of the future will change, but the face behind it will remain the same."

FREDERICK SEIDEL was born in St. Louis, Missouri, in 1936. He earned an undergraduate degree at Harvard University in 1957. He is the author of numerous collections of poetry, including *Ooga-Booga* (2006), winner of the *Los Angeles Times* Book Prize; *The Cosmos Trilogy* (2003); and *Going Fast* (1998), all from Farrar, Straus and Giroux.

CHARLES SIMIC was born in Belgrade, Yugoslavia, in 1938. "I'm sort of the product of history," he told an interviewer. "Hitler and Stalin were my travel agents." In 1953 he, his brother, and his mother joined his father in the United States. He was drafted into the U.S. Army in 1961 and published his first full-length collection of poems, *What the Grass Says,* in 1967, the year after he graduated from New York University. Since then he has published twenty books of poetry, among them *My Noiseless Entourage* (Harcourt, 2005), *Selected Poems: 1963–2003* (for which he received the 2005 International Griffin Poetry Prize), *The Voice at 3:00 A.M.: Selected Late and New Poems* (2003), *Jackstraws* (1999), *Hotel Insomnia* (1992), and *The World Doesn't End: Prose Poems* (1990), for which he received the Pulitzer Prize. A new book, *That Little Something,* will be published by Harcourt next spring. He was guest editor of *The Best American Poetry 1992.*

Of "Listen," Simic writes: "I always wondered who works in these places where they manufacture bombs, cages to put prisoners in, clubs to beat them over the head, and all the other gadgets of death they use in wartime? What is their night shift like, and so forth. . . . That's where the poem came from."

PATTI SMITH was born in Chicago, Illinois, in 1946. She is a poet and performer whose last book of poetry, *Auguries of Innocence,* was published by Ecco Press. On July 10, 2005, she was awarded the Commander of Arts and Letters from the French Ministry of Culture. In March 2007 she was inducted into the Rock and Roll Hall of Fame. She has a son and daughter and lives in New York City.

Of "Tara," Patti Smith writes: "On April 16, 2007, it snowed in Virginia. That same morning a young man opened fire in the halls and classes of Virginia Tech, killing thirty-two students and faculty before turning the gun on himself. My niece Simone attends classes there and her mother, Tara, waited alone at her farm for news from her daughter. I reached Tara moments after Simone called in, unharmed but searching for missing classmates. Tara expressed her feelings mixed with awe for the unexpected snow and the appearance of a family of deer.

"The poem came quickly as we said good-bye."

R. T. SMITH was born in Washington, D.C., in 1947 and was raised and educated in Georgia and North Carolina. For many years he served as Alumni Writer-in-Residence at Auburn University. He is the author of several books, including *The Hollow Log Lounge* (Illinois University

Press, 2003), *Uke Rivers Delivers: Stories* (Louisiana State University Press, 2006), and *Outlaw Style* (Arkansas, 2007). He edits *Shenandoah: The Washington and Lee University Review* and lives in Rockbridge County, Virginia, with his wife, the poet Sarah Kennedy.

Of "Pentecost," Smith writes: "Every time I see, read about, or even think about people handling snakes as an exercise of faith, I get a chill that's not easy to dispel, but I also sharpen the focus of my attention and ponder the act. I continue to be stunned and bewildered that 'Signs Following' believers will engage in this dangerous practice, but at the same time, I envy them their fierce conviction, their outlaw willingness to violate convention and statutes in order to get closer to the source of the Word. I suppose psychologists still call my conundrum 'ambivalence,' and I've tried several times to express this blend of envy and loathing in a poem, trying also to convey the sound and feel of both the snakes and the worshippers. With 'Pentecost,' I hope I'm getting close."

DAVE SNYDER was born in New Haven, Connecticut, in 1978, and grew up in Seattle. He holds degrees in geology and English and works as a secretary and a gardener in Chicago.

Snyder writes: "'Hexagon: On Truth' began after I read two pieces of nonfiction in quick succession: *Here There Be Dragons* by Margaret Wertheim, an essay from 2002 about the University of Arizona Mirror Lab, and *The Life of the Bee*, a singularly beautiful book of natural philosophy by Nobel laureate Maurice Maeterlinck first published in 1901. I was struck by both writers' ability to approach science with erudite wonder. With guidance from my friend and mentor Dan Beachy-Quick, 'Hexagon: On Truth' evolved as a hybrid of multiple sources and disparate images. Dan and I were surprised by the strange, bodiless voice the poem developed in this mixing of contemporary and antique science."

LISA RUSS SPAAR was born in Elizabeth, New Jersey, in 1956. She is the author of *Satin Cash: Poems* (Persea Books, 2008), *Blue Venus: Poems* (Persea Books, 2004), and *Glass Town: Poems* (Red Hen Press, 1999), for which she received a Rona Jaffe Award for Emerging Women Writers in 2000. She is the editor of *All That Mighty Heart: London Poems* (University of Virginia Press, 2008) and *Acquainted with the Night: Insomnia Poems* (Columbia University Press, 1999). She is the director of the Area Program in Poetry Writing at the University of Virginia, where she is an associate professor of English.

Of "Cricket," Spaar writes: "When I wake with my insomnia, I am struck by how I do not possess the things slowly taking shape myopically around me—tremble of water in a glass, neon clock face, closet, eyeglasses, window lattices—any more than I possess myself, any self. I am just a body, a thing, we are all things in the dark. But a voice is not a thing. It is bodiless (though often shaped by a body), a beyonding—it is the utterance primordial behind all life, the lyric: infant squall, love cry, keen of surprise, sorrow, wind, soul, chagrin. Cricket-song strikes me as particularly prophetic, stalking the interstices and backs of things, hawking winter, a note of paradise lingering in a chord that becomes more haunting as we pitch toward the solstice. This music forms the vigilant descant of my night watches."

KATHRYN STARBUCK was born in Algona, Iowa, in 1939. She wrote her first poem at the age of sixty and began publishing widely. Her first collection, *Griefmania,* was published by the Sheep Meadow Press in 2006. She is a former political journalist and commentator and for many years was the editor of the Milford (NH) *Cabinet* newspaper. She has edited two collections of her late husband George Starbuck's poems. She lives in Tuscaloosa, Alabama.

Of "The Shoe," Starbuck writes: "The postman rang once on August 15, 2006, the tenth anniversary of my husband's death, and handed me an acceptance letter for 'The Shoe' from *Harvard Review.* What was this? I telephoned *HR* and asked them to read the poem to me. Clearly it was my work. But I did not remember writing the poem. I did not remember submitting it. I asked them to send me a copy of the poem. I still have no memory of writing or submitting it.

"I tore my house upside down looking for that poem. Had Don Share and Christina Thompson at *Harvard Review* not rescued it, the poem would have been consigned to oblivion. I've never found it. Not in my dozens of boxes of hard copy revisions—my poems customarily go through as many as forty stops and starts—not in my computer files, not behind my couch. In the delirious aftermath of manic creative ecstasy, I must have submitted my raw and only copy of 'The Shoe'— exactly as printed here—then buried the delicious experience somewhere deep inside my wide wealthy memory where I've no doubt it still sings."

ALAN SULLIVAN was born in New York City in 1948 and grew up in the Bay Ridge neighborhood of Brooklyn. He attended Trinity College in

Hartford, Connecticut. He has written the science-fiction novels *Elixir* and *The Pearls of Poritrin*, a verse drama (*Gluntr in the Earth*), and a sailing memoir (*Cruising with Catullus*), in addition to poems (*Man Overboard*). He has lived in Minnesota and North Dakota and currently resides in Dania Beach, Florida.

Of "Divide and Conquer," Sullivan writes: "After I was diagnosed with leukemia, I corresponded with a leading cancer researcher, and when I wrote this villanelle the following year, I sent him a copy. He wrote back that my description of cancer was clinically accurate to such a degree that he could hardly believe a layman had composed it. So I would like to dedicate the poem to Doctor Terry Hamblin of Bournemouth, England."

CHAD SWEENEY was born in 1970 in Norman, Oklahoma, and has lived in San Francisco since 1994. His recent collections of poetry include *Arranging the Blaze* (Anhinga Press, 2009), *An Architecture* (BlazeVOX, 2007), and *A Mirror to Shatter the Hammer* (Tarpaulin Sky, 2006). He edits *Parthenon West Review* with David Holler and has translated (with Mojdeh Marashi, from Farsi) *Arghavaan, the Selected Poems of H. E. Sayeh*. He lives on Potrero Hill with his wife, the poet Jennifer K. Sweeney.

Sweeney writes: "I wrote 'The Sentence' while staring at a bird marsh. I've always been interested in the communication between text and the plastic arts, and this image rippled mysteriously across the marsh—the bones of Marcel Duchamp stretched into a long sentence, as both lingual structure and sculpture, one of Duchamp's *readymades* pieced together from found objects. The drama takes place at noon, motionless noon crouched into negative capability, when the world is worlding, and forms pulse in a combinative protean grammar. Several months later I wrote about the bird marsh while staring at a junkyard."

MARY SZYBIST was born in Williamsport, Pennsylvania, in 1970. Her book, *Granted* (Alice James Books, 2003), won the Great Lakes Colleges Association's New Writers Award. She teaches at Lewis & Clark College in Portland, Oregon.

Szybist writes: "I began writing 'The Troubadours etc.' shortly following my move to the Pacific Northwest in 2004. That summer my husband, Jerry, and I drove from Ohio to Oregon. The Midwest I had been living in for almost a decade slowly disappeared behind us, and as it did, I let my mind wander.

"I was accompanied, in these meanderings, by troubadours. I had been reading them and thinking about the relationship between language and desire. Even though Jerry & I are both poets, it seems strangely beside the point to attempt 'the eloquence of love.' But I find myself with a certain nostalgia. It's not that the troubadours had everything right—far from it—but rather that I sometimes long for such uncompromising ideas about love and such faith in language to compel it. After the trip was over, I thought of the long, leisurely silences we shared as we moved across the seemingly endless American highway, and I somehow wanted to speak into them."

JAMES TATE was born in Kansas City, Missouri, in 1943. In 1966, when he won the Yale Younger Poets Prize for his book *The Lost Pilot,* he was among the youngest poets ever thus honored. His *Selected Poems* (Wesleyan University Press, 1991) received the Pulitzer Prize for poetry in 1992, and *Worshipful Company of Fletchers* (Ecco Press, 1994) won the National Book Award two years later. Among his other books are *Return to the City of White Donkeys* (Ecco, 2004) and *The Route as Briefed* (University of Michigan Press, 1999). He teaches at the University of Massachusetts in Amherst and was the guest editor of *The Best American Poetry 1997.* On the strength of the poem Charles Wright chose for this year's anthology, Tate has agreed to serve as the national security adviser to the series editor and staff of *The Best American Poetry.*

NATASHA TRETHEWEY was born in Gulfport, Mississippi, in 1966. She is author of three collections of poetry, *Domestic Work* (Graywolf Press, 2000), *Bellocq's Ophelia* (Graywolf, 2002), and *Native Guard (*Houghton Mifflin, 2006) for which she won the Pulitzer Prize. At Emory University, she is a professor of English and holds the Phillis Wheatley Distinguished Chair in Poetry.

Of "On Captivity," Trethewey writes: "When I read the lines quoted as the poem's epigraph, I was struck by how the imagery of the captivity narrative echoed the illustrated scene that presents Adam and Eve, in their newly realized nakedness, covered by leaves. Because the conquerors made use of the written word to claim land inhabited by native people, I found the detail of settlers forced to cover themselves with pages torn from books a compelling irony."

LEE UPTON was born in St. Johns, Michigan, in 1953. She is the author of ten books, most recently a book of poetry, *Undid in the Land of Undone* (New Issues Poetry & Prose, 2007), and a literary study of how poets claim their distinctiveness, *Defensive Measures* (Bucknell University Press,

2005). She is a professor of English and the writer-in-residence at Lafayette College in Pennsylvania.

Of "Thomas Hardy," Upton writes: "Years ago I was in a class in which the teacher told us she wished Thomas Hardy had stuck to writing novels and never took up poetry. I was stunned. Who would want to be without Hardy's poetry? I can't read 'During Wind and Rain' without a sudden rushing sensation—a frightening intuition of mortality perhaps only possible to experience in a burst before the mind draws back. The poet of horrific loss and suffocating regret, Hardy is also a poet of that underrated emotion: pity. In rehearsing death, he rehearsed pity—repeatedly. Of course, there is an irony attached to his work. Out of his portrayals of disappointment and failure, he makes poetry of absolute mastery, poetry capable of piercing even a stupefied heart. It seems impossible to measure how he does it, how he plunges us so quickly into the depths of pity for his people and then elevates us into a new sense of the immensity of living a human life—before we snap back into our simpler, single selves once again."

DARA WIER was born in New Orleans, Louisiana, in 1949. Her recent books include *Remnants of Hannah* (Wave Books, 2006) and *Reverse Rapture* (Verse Press, 2005). She is a member of the poetry faculty and director of the MFA program for poets and writers at the University of Massachusetts in Amherst. She is also codirector of the Juniper Initiative for Literary Arts and Action. With Guy Pettit and Emily Pettit, she edits and publishes chapbooks and broadsides for Factory Hollow Press.

Wier writes: "'Faithful' was written while I was under an elegiac spell. I needed to keep reading and writing to keep away unbidden, private thoughts, to exchange my so-called ideas for those of others. Any manner of reading or writing would help, neutral or objective, highly subjective, combative reading, skeptical reading, friendly reading, eager reading, reading in which each word is savored, reading in which each letter is suddenly a fantastic monster, reading fast, very slow going reading, reading for what's there on the page, reading passively, reading aggressively, reading haphazardly, reading willfully.

"No one ever really said How Do I Know What I Think Until I See What I Say, or at least it is beginning to seem so. Last time I heard this quoted, someone said Joe DiMaggio said it. It was on the radio. A book was being discussed.

"In other words, how does art act to galvanize one's brain activity vs. imagination present and/or future thoughts, actions, behavior, emotions, etc., its character as action and proceedings, never static, never statically defined, faithful to its tendencies and inclinations.

"To address someone or something, unnamed and unknowable, is perhaps poetry's most violent, shattering, quintessential gift to us.

"And so I took to writing fourteen-line length poems in order to step into a very deep channel of tradition, to keep step with timing of this perfect length, to remove myself from the confines of the form established in my book *Reverse Rapture.*"

C. K. WILLIAMS was born in Newark, New Jersey, in 1936. His most recent book of poetry is his *Collected Poems,* which appeared in 2006, published by Farrar, Straus and Giroux. He has published nine other books of poetry, the most recent of which, *The Singing,* won the National Book Award for 2003; his previous book, *Repair,* was awarded the 2000 Pulitzer Prize. Both were also published by Farrar, Straus and Giroux. He teaches in the creative writing program at Princeton University.

Of "Light," Williams writes: "I'd wanted for many years to do something with Dante's mysterious description of characters in the *Divine Comedy* as '. . . the life of . . .' I'd also wanted, from the time my wife and I visited Africa the year before the poem began to take shape, to find a way to write something about the experience of that single bat among tens of thousands seeming to look me in the eye, to *notice* me. It seemed important to acknowledge the strange and profound sense of communion I sensed between us.

"Then as I woke one morning, looked out the window, and saw our drought-parched maple shining with evaporating raindrops, the word *uncountable* came to my mind, and along with it the cadence that drove 'silvery glitterings' before it, then an intuition of the rhythms of shape of the poem.

"It took another month to get the rest of it right, but I remember it as a very pleasant month: the poem is one of those the labor for which generated meanings and musics I wouldn't have thought were there until they were revealed."

FRANZ WRIGHT was born in Vienna in 1953. He is currently Ziskind Poet-in-Residence at Brandeis University. He received the 2004 Pulitzer Prize in poetry for his collection *Walking to Martha's Vineyard* (Knopf, 2003). His most recent books are *God's Silence* (2006) and *Earlier Poems* (2007), both from Knopf. "Passing Scenes (While Reading Basho)" is from a new collection called *Wheeling Motel* that will be published in fall 2009.

Wright writes: "'Passing Scenes (While Reading Basho)' concludes with a play on Basho's famous Kyoto haiku (though a seagull seemed to me a more appropriate bird; nightingales don't frequent New York City). I'd been carrying around in the back of my head these lines about missing New York even when in New York for the past ten years or so, and was pleased they finally found a home in this poem. And recently, reading Don DeLillo's *Falling Man,* I was amazed and delighted to discover the same idea—minus the seagull—had occurred at some point to him. It's wonderful to think that for years, without knowing it, I was secretly sharing this image with that very great author."

LYNN XU was born in Shanghai in 1982. She coedits Canarium Books and works as an independent curator and artist assistant. She is the author of one chapbook, *June* (Corollary Press, 2006). Anne Carson chose the poem anthologized here as the winner of the Greg Grummer Poetry Award from *Phoebe* magazine. Xu lives in New York City and Oaxaca, Mexico.

Xu writes: "'Language exists . . .' is the last section of a three-part poem called 'Say You Will Die for Me,' which is also the title poem of my first manuscript. The nature of incantation, wish making, the degrees of abstraction necessary in order for an idea to appear real, and the tremendous sadness involved in an idea, when it is fulfilled, were, I think, on my mind "

C. DALE YOUNG was born in 1969 and grew up in the Caribbean and south Florida. He was educated at Boston College (BS 1991) and the University of Florida (MFA 1993, MD 1997). He currently practices medicine full-time, administers his own medical practice, edits poetry for *New England Review,* and teaches in the Warren Wilson College MFA Program for Writers. His poetry collections are *The Day Underneath the Day* (Northwestern University Press, 2001) and *The Second Person* (Four Way Books, 2007). He is currently at work on a third manuscript of poems titled *TORN.*

Of "Sepsis," Young writes: "From July of 1997 through June of 1998, I worked as a Medical/Surgical Intern. During that year, I grew from being one who simply held a medical degree into a full-fledged physician. It was a difficult and painful year filled with triumphs and great disappointments, a year filled with an incredible amount of learning and an incredible amount of fatigue. Unfortunately, it was also the year in which I learned what every physician must learn, the consequence of failure. Although 'Sepsis' is an amalgam of experiences I had during that year, it is very much a testament to the thoughts and feelings I have carried forward into the rest of my life as a physician. Every physician must, at some point, face the fact that they are human, that they are not perfect. At the same time, anything less than perfection can mean failure. I began this poem with the hopes it would allow me some kind of psychological respite. In this, I was terribly wrong."

DAVID YOUNG was born in Davenport, Iowa, in 1936. Among his recent publications are *Black Lab* (Alfred A. Knopf, 2006), *Six Modernist Moments in Poetry* (Iowa, 2006), *The Poetry of Petrarch* (Farrar, Straus and Giroux, 2004), and *Out on the Autumn River: Selected Poems of Du Mu* (with Jiann I. Lin, Rager Media, Inc., 2007). Forthcoming: *Du Fu: A Life in Poetry* (Knopf, 2008) and *Paul Celan: From Threshold to Threshold* (Eastern Washington University Press, 2008). He is the Emeritus Longman Professor of English and creative writing at Oberlin College and is the editor of *FIELD* magazine and Oberlin College Press.

Young writes: "Over the past few years I have found myself writing occasional poems, poems that respond to a specific moment—e.g., the Terri Schiavo case, the death of a friend, the experience of being moved by rereading a favorite poet—by turning to the sonnet. I think this is because I have translated so many sonnets (Rilke, then Petrarch) and memorized others (Shakespeare, Donne, Hopkins) while on my dog walks. The form is right at hand for me, and it's an accommodating one, adaptable to many subjects and moments, as poets like Petrarch and Shakespeare certainly understood. In this case I had a sudden moment of insight into the way we both do and don't want to acknowledge and remember our war dead.

"As readers will see, I prefer not to rhyme my sonnets fully, but to let possibilities of rhyme and off-rhyme arise and unfold as the occasion seems to dictate. To me, our flickering awareness of the war dead is similar to the flickering of formal possibility around a contemporary use of a traditional form, though the former is obviously painful and the latter mostly playful."

DEAN YOUNG was born in Columbia, Pennsylvania, in 1955. He has published nine books of poems, most recently *embryoyo* (Believer Books, 2007) and *Primitive Mentor* (University of Pittsburgh Press, 2008). He teaches at the University of Iowa Writers' Workshop and last year received an award in literature from the American Academy of Arts and Letters, so he tells everyone he got an Academy Award.

Of "No Forgiveness Ode," Young writes: "This poem always spooked me a little. Essentially it began as a rhyming list but it seems to develop a more central concern which I'd just as soon know nothing about. Well, as I've said to my students, the imagination is the highest accomplishment of consciousness and empathy is the highest accomplishment of the imagination."

KEVIN YOUNG was born in Lincoln, Nebraska, in 1970, but moved to Boston before he was one year old; his family hails from Louisiana. He is the author of six books of poetry, and the editor of four others. *Jelly Roll: A Blues* (Alfred A. Knopf, 2003) was awarded the Paterson Poetry Prize, and *For the Confederate Dead* (Knopf, 2007) received the Quill Award in Poetry in 2007. *Dear Darkness* will appear in fall 2008. He is Atticus Haygood Professor of creative writing and English and curator of the Raymond Danowski Poetry Library at Emory University.

Young writes: "The sequence 'Book of Hours' began at the Squaw Valley Community of Writers in California, near where the Donner Party met its fate. In the weeklong workshop, everyone writes and brings a poem a day, including the workshop leaders; the first few poems in the sequence came from that process, which I found quite freeing. As such, the places in the poem are thus literal in some sense, but may also be thought of as the Valley from the spirituals the slaves sang or the Mountaintop that Langston Hughes and later Martin Luther King spoke of facing. It is ascent the poem seeks.

"The title 'Book of Hours' is taken from the medieval devotionals that were at first for those who could afford them, and which then became more and more common; in them prayers were offered for each liturgical hour of the day (such as evening vespers), as well as illuminations depicting not just biblical scenes but everyday ones (such as harvesting). The last line of the poem—'Why not sing'—provides as close to a summary of my poetic philosophy as I can imagine ever having."

MAGAZINES WHERE THE POEMS
WERE FIRST PUBLISHED

32 Poems, eds. Deborah Ager and John Poch. Texas Tech University, Lubbock, TX 79409-3091.

ABZ, eds. John McKernan and James Raffle. PO Box 2746, Huntington, WV 25727-2746.

AGNI, poetry eds. Lynne Potts and Jay Deshpande. Boston University, 236 Bay State Rd., Boston, MA 02215.

American Poetry Review, eds. Stephen Berg, David Bonanno, and Elizabeth Scanlon. 1700 Sansom St., Suite 800, Philadelphia, PA 19103.

The American Scholar, poetry ed. Langdon Hammer. 1606 New Hampshire Avenue NW, Washington, DC 20009.

Barrow Street, eds. Lorna Blake, Patricia Carlin, Peter Covino, and Melissa Hotchkiss. PO Box 1831, New York, NY 10156.

Bird Dog, ed. Sarah Mangold. 1535 32nd Ave., Apt. C, Seattle, WA 98122.

Brilliant Corners, ed. Sascha Feinstein. Lycoming College, Williamsport, PA 17701.

Crazyhorse, eds. Carol Ann Davis and Garrett Doherty. Department of English, College of Charleston, 66 George St., Charleston, SC 29424.

FIELD, eds. David Young and David Walker. Oberlin College Press, 50 N. Professor St., Oberlin, OH 44074.

Five Points, eds. David Bottoms and Megan Sexton. Georgia State University, PO Box 3999, Atlanta, GA 30302-3999.

Fulcrum, co-eds.-in-chief Philip Nikolayev and Katia Kapovich. 421 Huron Avenue, Cambridge, MA 02138.

Gulf Coast, poetry eds. Kent Shaw and Paul Otremba. Department of English, University of Houston, Houston, TX 77204–3013.

Harvard Review, ed. Christina Thompson. Lamont Library, Harvard University, Cambridge, MA 02138.

The Hudson Review, ed. Paula Dietz. 684 Park Ave., New York, NY 10021.

The Iowa Review, ed. David Hamilton. 308 EPB, The University of Iowa, Iowa City, IA 52242.

The Kenyon Review, poetry ed. David Baker. 102 W. Wiggin St., Gambier, OH 43022. www.kenyonreview.org

LIT, poetry ed. Graeme Bezanson. The New School Writing Program, Room 514, 66 West 12th St., New York, NY 10011.

London Review of Books, ed. Mary-Kay Wilmers. 28 Little Russell St., London WC1A 2HN.

Lyric, founding ed. Mira Rosenthal; ed., Nathanial Perry; senior ed., Eve Grubin. PO Box 2494, Bloomington, IN 47402.

Meridian. University of Virginia, PO Box 400145, Charlottesville, VA 22904–4145.

The Nation, poetry ed. Peter Gizzi. 33 Irving Place, New York, NY 10003.

New American Writing, eds. Maxine Chernoff and Paul Hoover. 369 Molino Ave., Mill Valley, CA 94941

New England Review, poetry ed. C. Dale Young. Middlebury College, Middlebury, VT 05753.

The New York Review of Books, ed. Robert Silvers. 1755 Broadway, 5th floor, New York, NY 10019.

The New Yorker, poetry ed. Paul Muldoon. 4 Times Square, New York, NY 10036.

Notre Dame Review, eds. John Matthias and William O'Rourke. 840 Flanner Hall, University of Notre Dame, Notre Dame, IN 46556.

The Paris Review, poetry eds. Meghan O'Rourke and Charles Simic. 62 White St., New York, NY 10013.

Phoebe, poetry ed. Wade Fletcher. MSN 2D6, George Mason University, 4400 University Drive, Fairfax, VA 22030-4444.

Ploughshares, poetry ed. John Skoyles. Emerson College, 120 Boylston St., Boston, MA 02116-4624.

Poetry, ed. Christian Wiman. 444 North Michigan Ave., Suite 1850, Chicago, IL 60611.

Prairie Schooner, ed.-in-chief Hilda Raz. 201 Andrews Hall, PO Box 880334, Lincoln, NE 68588-0334.

Quarterly West, poetry eds. Kathryn Cowles and Stacey Kidd. 255 South Central Campus Drive, Rm. 3500, University of Utah, Salt Lake City, UT 84112-9109.

Raritan, ed.-in-chief Jackson Lears. 31 Mine St., New Brunswick, NJ 08903.

Rivendell, ed. Sebastian Matthews. PO Box 9594, Asheville, NC 28815.

Runes, eds. C. B. Follett and Susan Terris. Arctos Press: http://members.aol.com/runes/

Sentence, ed. Brian Clements. Firewheel Editions, Box 7, Western Connecticut State University, 181 White St., Danbury, CT 06810.

Sewanee Theological Review, poetry ed. Greg Williamson. The University of the South, School of Theology, Box 46-W, Sewanee TN 37383-0001.

The Sienese Shredder, eds. Brice Brown and Trevor Winkfield. 344 West 23rd St. #4D, New York, NY 10011. www.sienese-shredder.com

The Southern Review, ed. Jeanne Leiby. Louisiana State University, Old President's House, Baton Rouge, LA 70803.

storySouth, poetry ed. Dan Albergotti. www.storysouth.com

Subtropics, poetry ed. Sidney Wade. PO Box 112075, 4008 Turlington Hall, University of Florida, Gainesville, FL 32611-2075.

Verse, eds. Brian Henry and Andrew Zawacki. English Department, University of Richmond, Richmond, VA 23173.

Virginia Quarterly Review, ed. Ted Genoways, poetry chair David Lee Rubin. University of Virginia, One West Range, Box 400223, Charlottesville, VA 22904-4223. www.vqronline.org

VOLT, ed. Gillian Conoley. PO Box 657, Corte Madera, CA 94976.

ACKNOWLEDGMENTS

The series editor wishes to thank Mark Bibbins for his invaluable assistance. I am grateful as well to Jill Baron, James Cummins, Judith Hall, Stacey Harwood, Jennifer Michael Hecht, Richard Howard, Sarah Ruth Jacobs, Kathleen Ossip, Michael Schiavo, Benjamin Taylor, and Matthew Zapruder. Warm thanks go, as always, to Glen Hartley and Lynn Chu of Writers' Representatives, and to Alexis Gargagliano, my editor, and Jennifer Bernard, Daniel Cuddy, Anna deVries, Molly Dorozenski, and Erich Hobbing of Scribner.

Grateful acknowledgment is made of the magazines in which these poems first appeared and the magazine editors who selected them. A sincere attempt has been made to locate all copyright holders. Unless otherwise noted, copyright to the poems is held by the individual poets

Tom Andrews: "Evening Song" from *Random Symmetries: The Collected Poems of Tom Andrews*. Copyright © 2002 by the Estate of Tom Andrews. Reprinted by permission of Oberlin College Press. Also appeared in *Rivendell*.

Ralph Angel: "Exceptions and Melancholies" from *Exceptions and Melancholies: Poems 1986–2006*. Copyright © 2006 by Ralph Angel. Reprinted by permission of Sarabande Books. Also appeared in *Runes*.

Rae Armantrout: "Framing" appeared in *The Nation*. Reprinted by permission of the poet.

John Ashbery: "Pavane pour Helen Twelvetrees" from *A Worldly Country*. Copyright © 2007 by John Ashbery. Reprinted by permission of Ecco/HarperCollins. Also appeared in *The New York Review of Books*.

Joshua Beckman: poem beginning with "The canals. The liquor coming through" from *Shake*. Copyright © 2006 by Joshua Beckman. Reprinted by permission of Wave Books. Also appeared in *Bird Dog*.

Marvin Bell: "Poseur" from *Mars Being Red*. Copyright © 2007 by Marvin Bell. Reprinted by permission of Copper Canyon Press. Also appeared in *The Iowa Review*.

Charles Bernstein: "Ku(na)hay" appeared in *Barrow Street*. Reprinted by permission of the poet.

Ciaran Berry: "Electrocuting an Elephant" from *The Sphere of Birds*.

Russ Spaar. Reprinted by permission of Persea Books. Also appeared in *Meridian*.

Kathryn Starbuck: "The Shoe" appeared in *Harvard Review*. Reprinted by permission of the poet.

Alan Sullivan: "Divide and Conquer" first appeared in *The Hudson Review*. Reprinted by permission of the poet.

Chad Sweeney: "The Sentence" first appeared in *New American Writing*. Reprinted by permission of the poet.

Mary Szybist: "The Troubadors etc." first appeared in *Meridian*. Reprinted by permission of the poet.

James Tate: "National Security" first appeared in *VOLT*. Reprinted by permission of the poet.

Natasha Trethewey: "On Captivity" first appeared in *Five Points*. Reprinted by permission of the poet.

Lee Upton: "Thomas Hardy" from *Undid in the Land of Undone*. Copyright © 2007 by Lee Upton. Reprinted by permission of New Issues Press. Also appeared in *Barrow Street*.

Dara Wier: "Faithful" first appeared in *The American Poetry Review*. Reprinted by permission of the poet.

C. K. Williams: "Light" first appeared in *The New Yorker*. Reprinted by permission of the poet.

Franz Wright: "Passing Scenes (While Reading Basho)" first appeared in *FIELD*. Reprinted by permission of the poet.

Lynn Xu: "Language exists because. . ." first appeared in *Phoebe*. Reprinted by permission of the poet.

C. Dale Young: "Sepsis" first appeared in *The Virginia Quarterly Review*. Reprinted by permission of the poet.

David Young: "The Dead from Iraq" first appeared in *ABZ: A Poetry Magazine*. Reprinted by permission of the poet.

Dean Young: "No Forgiveness Ode" from *embryoyo*. Copyright © 2007 by Dean Young. Reprinted by permission of Believer Books. Also appeared in *The Paris Review* (as "Poem without Forgiveness").

Kevin Young: excerpt from "Book of Hours" first appeared in *Poetry*. Reprinted by permission of the poet.